Oxted 2000

Oxted, Hurst Green and District
A History and Guide for the Millennium
by Mary Alderton

Published by Oxted Parish Council

Published by Oxted Parish Council 1999

ISBN 0 9536221 0 X

© Mary Alderton

The rights of Mary Alderton to be identified as author of this work have been asserted by her in accordance with the Copyright, Designs and Patents Act 1988.

Also by Mary Alderton: *The Blue Guide to Sweden*

Illustrations
Cover painting by *Patricia Hall*
Photographs by *Paul Davies*
Additional photographs by *Mary Alderton*
Line drawings by *Chris Sorensen*
Two old photographs from the Francis Frith Collection, Salisbury, SP3 5QP
Old postcards lent by The Stamp Shop, Oxted
Extract from the Domesday Book 1975 edition by Phillimore & Co Ltd., Chichester, PO20 6BG
Plan of St Mary's Church from Victoria County History

INTRODUCTION

This book is a celebration. At the start of the twenty-first century we look back over the history of the centuries which have gone before. The past explains how our community came to be what it is today. To explore the past is a great adventure and I want you to join all the households of Oxted and Hurst Green parish in this exploration. You will be able to relate to past events and see the buildings and countryside which are our legacy from the years gone by.

As well as remembering and reading about the past, this book is also about the future. The future is unknown, but reading this book will help us to appreciate events as they happen and enable us to understand the corner of the world in which we live. We are very fortunate to be able to live our lives among caring neighbours in a thriving town which is set in beautiful countryside. So please enjoy this book because it was written with you in mind.

If future historians refer to this book we hope that it helps towards an understanding of how we lived at the end of the twentieth century. We look forward to the twenty-first century with anticipation. May the Parish of Oxted and Hurst Green continue to be as inviting and prosperous as it is today.

Stanley Gibson
Chairman of the Millennium Committee,
Oxted and Hurst Green Parish Council
Chairman of Oxted Chamber of Commerce 1989-95

Members of Oxted Parish Council in the Year 2000

Anthony Cherrett, Chairman
Mrs Barbara Chandler
Keith Evans
Martin Fisher
Stanley Gibson
Michael Grimes
Mrs Barbara Harling
Mrs Elizabeth Parker
Mrs Jacqueline Reed
David Weightman
Mrs Karen Weightman

Mrs Grace Green, Clerk to the Council

Contents

Foreword

Chapter One   **Beginnings**

Position - The Land - Building Materials - The Old Road - The Stone Age to the Saxons - The Hundred's Knoll

Chapter Two   **The Middle Ages**

The Domesday Book - Surrey in the Domesday Book - The name Oxted - Life in Oxted - Buildings - St Mary's Church: Building History and the Church Today - *Manors of Oxted:* Oxted, Birsted, Broadham, Foyle, Stocketts - Watermills - *Old Oxted:* inns, hall houses, cottages - *Hurst Green - Broadham Green - Merle Common* -Tandridge - Limpsfield

Chapter Three   **Early Modern Times 16C-18C**

How the Town Grew: Houses, Farms and Families of the Seventeenth and Eighteenth Centuries, Watermills

Chapter Four   **The Nineteenth Century**

Before the Railway: Building Development, Industries - *The Oxted Railway - Buses - Development after the Railway - The Master Family:* The Churchyard of St Mary's - *Literary Figures in Oxted*

Chapter Five   **The Twentieth Century**

New Building - Memorials in the Churchyard of St Mary's - The Nightingales of Foyle Riding - Memories from between the Wars - Oxted in World War II - Notable Residents - Lives of Local People - Post-war Development - The 1990s

Chapter Six   **Oxted today and into the Millennium**

Schools: Oxted School, St Mary's, Moor House, Laverock, Downs Way, Limpsfield Grange, Hurst Green County Primary, Holland Junior - *Churches:* St Mary's, All Saints, Church of the Peace of God, St John's, Methodist, other religious communities - *Organisations:* Link Association, charitable associations, other interests - *Health and Leisure - Entertainment*

Internet Sites

Further Reading

Oxted Village in 1905, showing the unsurfaced road, and the Wheatsheaf before it acquired its half-timbering

Foreword

This history and guide covering Oxted, Hurst Green and district is published by Oxted Parish Council and funded by the Millennium Commission. It is distributed to every household in the Parish as a memento of the Millennium.

This book is written from the point of view of someone who wishes to know the story behind the main features which can be seen today. In this way it is a guide as well as a history.

The book would not have seen the light of day without the driving force of Mr Stanley Gibson of Oxted Parish Council who had the vision to start the project and see it through. Also from the parish council, Councillor Mrs Karen Weightman and parish clerk Mrs Grace Green gave considerable capable assistance. A special word of gratitude goes to Mr Peter Gray for his help and his permission to make use of the immensely detailed information in his *Inventory of Buildings of Historic Interest in Oxted*.

Grateful thanks are also due to all those generous people who gave so lavishly of their information, expertise, memories and other knowledge, and above all, their valuable time. Those who are not mentioned in the text include: Jennifer Caswell, Melinda Cherrett, Dr R.J. Cockerill, Illtyd Gray-Jones, Barbara Harling, Mrs C. Howard, Peggy Kaye, Warwick Keeson, Gavin Grossmith, John Lea, M. Ludford, Mike Moss, Malcolm Page, D.J. Peaple, J.A. Pope, Kay Ridsdale, Alan Robertson and others whose names unfortunately I do not know. Without them this book would be much the poorer.

Mary Alderton

Meridian marker at Lovells' outfitters

Oxted from the North Downs

Chapter One

Beginnings

Although the written history of Oxted begins with the Domesday Book, the area was inhabited long before that, from the late Iron Age. The site and the nature of the land determined the type of settlement which would thrive and be viable through the centuries.

Position

Oxted is exactly on the **Greenwich Meridian** at 0° longitude and on 51°15' latitude. The Greenwich Meridian goes through Oxted School, across Bluehouse Lane, just slices the ends of Beatrice Road and Amy Road, crosses Station Road East at an oblique angle, through Paydens' chemists on one side and Lovells' outfitters on the other, where there is a marker in the window. The meridian then crosses the A25 main road just east of the railway bridge, and continues through Hurst Green, passing by the crossroads where Tanhouse Road meets Woodhurst Lane. Thus Old Oxted and most of New Oxted are in the west, while most of Hurst Green is in the east. Nowadays 'New' Oxted has been sandwiched between the M25 motorway and the A25. Old Oxted is to the south of the A25, while Hurst Green has grown up in the wake of the railway and today is closely linked to Oxted.

The Land

The town centre is situated on a narrow band of Lower Greensand which crosses Surrey from east to west. This Greensand strip widens out and becomes the valley of the River Wey in the west of the county. The parish straddles also a narrow strip of Gault Clay and then the broad sweep of the chalk of the North Downs to the north, while to the south is a wide band of Weald Clay. The so-called Pilgrims' Way from Winchester to Canterbury which passes to the north of Oxted was first mentioned as a name in the 18C, but was made common usage by romantically-minded Victorians. The track is in fact prehistoric and led along the foot of the chalk escarpment which would be less wet than the clay, and also as it faced south it would be dried by the sun. Some of the northern part of the parish is included in the Surrey Hills Area of Outstanding Natural Beauty, so designated in 1983.

The River Eden meanders through the town more or less north to south, eventually draining into the Medway. Though now largely disregarded except as a picturesque feature of gardens or fields, it was not so in the days when its water powered the mills which were vital to supply the daily bread of the inhabitants, and in far distant times of course this was the main water supply for all their needs.

Building Materials

Local building stone includes Godstone clunch which is chalky and produces rather small blocks. There is also ironstone which is hard to work but makes good walls with wide mortar bands and galletting (small stones inserted into the mortar). Sandstone was used later, but was almost as hard, so that mortar bands were again wide and galletting was used. This sandstone weathers to grey-green. Window jambs and angles had to be made of brick which was more amenable to elegant moulding and carving. Red bricks were made on Limpsfield Common up to the beginning of the 20C.

In addition of course there were trees to use, especially oak for the great timber-framed hall houses of the Middle Ages, since the southern part of the parish lay in the Weald, thickly forested in those days.

For roofing, tiles were made at Limpsfield in the Middle Ages. There was thatch too, which was a free by-product of farming, and Horsham stone slates (found in a wider area than Horsham itself) were used for more prestigious buildings and formed very heavy, thick slabs.

The Old Road by Hilaire Belloc (1904)

Belloc proposes the theory that the prehistoric trackway along the southern escarpment of the North Downs was a route from Dover, the obvious point of entry into the country from the continent, to the plain of Salisbury, with later a spur to Winchester, the seat of power in ancient Britain. He recounts how he and two friends walked along the whole length in a week. As they reached the railway cutting at the entrance to the Oxted tunnel, night fell and they stumbled along the railway track to find an inn. There they squabbled with a fellow traveller, spent the night, and the next day rejoined their route across Titsey Park.

The Stone Age to the Saxons

In the Surrey Greensand area archaeologists have found more flint tools from the **Middle Stone Age** (Mesolithic) than in other types of geological formation because the lighter density of vegetation on the sand made it easier for hunters to move around. Most of Surrey must have been well wooded however, to judge by the large numbers of place names containing 'wood' or 'hurst', not to mention those actually specifying the type of tree such as Oxted, 'the place of the oaks'. Oakwood and Ockley are other examples indicating oaks, and there are also many with 'ash'.

With the advent of the **Late Stone Age** (Neolithic) in about 3000BC hunters did not immediately turn from hunting to farming, but gradually adopted a more settled way of life. Flint tools began to be polished, and pottery was made, with designs which show that they were copied from woven baskets. We do not have in Surrey those other great indicators of the Neolithic, causewayed camps, and we have only one long barrow. Neolithic tools have been found mainly on chalk because these tools could not cope with clay and the sand was unproductive.

Anglo-Saxon gravestones beside St Mary's Church

During the **Bronze Age**, beginning about 1800BC, Surrey people seem to have been a peace-loving lot, for more bronze tools have been found than bronze weapons. The so-called Pilgrims' Way was probably established in the Bronze Age. Round barrows became the fashionable burial place and there are about 60 remaining in Surrey, though many have been destroyed. The knoll at Barrow Green now known as the Mount is not a barrow but was a fortified hill. Most of it is natural, but a ditch had been dug around it and the material from the ditch piled on top. It was excavated in 1869 by the Surrey Archaeological Society and there was no burial, but some worked flints were found. The word 'barrow' has been associated with the place at least since the 16C.

With the **Iron Age**, beginning about 500BC, the first Celtic peoples arrived - these were the earliest Britons. Along the Greensand escarpment they established several hill forts where all the people and animals could take refuge if attacked. Iron Age pottery found in Surrey shows different styles, which indicates a shifting population of different tribes. This tribal movement was perhaps the reason why no Roman town was ever established in Surrey as there was no settled nucleus on which to build. Because the area could be easily controlled from London the Romans did not bother to build a fort here either. However, we know that one Roman family had a villa at Titsey of which only a few stones now remain.

After the **Romans** had left and the **Saxons** began to settle and make themselves at home, many of today's villages were founded. It was the Saxons who gave Surrey its name - Suðre ge, the south kingdom (ð is the Saxon symbol for 'th'). When the Saxons became Christian in about the 7C, sometimes a lord or thegn would build a church which would become a meeting-point for his tenants and servants and so form the nucleus of a village. At the time of the Norman invasion Oxted was owned by Gytha, wife of Godwine the Earl of Wessex, and it is probable that Oxted's church had indeed such an aristocratic foundress.

When the M25 motorway was being constructed, archaeologists had a look at the excavations before it was all covered again. Lesley Ketteringham reported on the findings for the section from Godstone to the Kent border in *Surrey Archaeological Collections, Vol. 80*, and found that the area had been cultivated by Late Iron Age and Romano-British people. There was evidence of some small farms possibly from before Norman times, and they had been farmed ever since. But it was odd that there was not very much activity between the time the Romans left and the advent of the Middle Ages. The fact that worked flints were not discovered illustrated that these early peoples preferred to live on higher ground, where flint tools are indeed found.

The Hundred's Knoll on the A25

> ### The Hundred's Knoll
>
> This hillock in the parish of Tandridge on the north side of the A25 near Tandridge Lane bears the Moot Stone, with a plaque commemorating its days as the site of the Hundred's Courts held from Saxon times to the 18C. In 1720 it is known that constables were elected here. In the 17C the name was recorded as 'Hundredsnow', presumably a corruption of 'Hundred's Knoll', and later still developed into 'Undersnow'.
>
> The inscription reads: ON THIS HILL THE HUNDRED'S KNOLL (KNOWN LATER AS 'UNDERSNOW') THE SAXON TYTHINGMEN FROM THE SURROUNDING VILLAGES OF THE HUNDRED OF TANDRIDGE MET AS THE FIRST LOCAL GOVERNMENT AND COURT IN THE GODSTONE RURAL DISTRICT.
>
> When Tandridge District was created in 1973 the new name was suggested by James Batley, the chairman of the Bourne Society for local history, because the boundaries of the new district were very similar to those of the old Tandridge Hundred.

The period before the Battle of Hastings in 1066 laid the foundations for a new age. With the coming of the Normans, a small settlement began to grow up on the site of Old Oxted. The pace of change was in those days extremely slow and it was many centuries before anything like a thriving village came into being.

The Mount at Barrow Green

Chapter Two

The Middle Ages

As with so many towns, the recorded history of Oxted begins with the Domesday Book. Social changes were afoot, brought about by the advent of the Normans, and the feudal system. They tended to try to keep their subjects happy by retaining many of the old ways which affected everyday life, laying the foundation for peace and prosperity while imposing their methods of government. The medieval period is when Oxted began to establish itself as an integrated community, and in its later stages, during the 15C and 16C, some of the most picturesque and interesting buildings were constructed.

The Domesday Book

The Domesday Book was a survey carried out for William the Conqueror in 1086, with corrections in 1087, written in Latin as were all official documents. Essex, Suffolk and Norfolk are contained in one volume, the rest, except for some northern counties, in another. The original manuscripts are in the Public Record Office, and the rendering shown here is from 1783, when the government of the time had 1250 copies of the books printed, using a type specially made for the task. This was a huge undertaking which cost £18,000 and took 16 years.

Extract from the 1783 edition of the Domesday Book mentioning 'Acstede' (line two)

Surrey in the Domesday Book

There were five royal manors in Surrey - Godalming, Kingston, Wallington, Woking and Reigate, and one manor was held by a bishop at Farnham. The rest were held by various lords and abbeys, and here in Oxted and Godstone the lord was Eustace of Boulogne who owned large tracts elsewhere as well. (Limpsfield belonged to Battle Abbey.) Peasantry were in two main classes: cottagers and villeins - villeins had more rights than cottagers.

Churches were founded by all sorts of different people, kings, bishops, or local lords including late Saxon thegns (lords) who had become Christian. Gytha, as explained in Chapter One, probably founded the church in Oxted. She was married to Godwine, Earl of Wessex, who had been the most powerful man in England in the reign of Edward the Confessor, and she was the mother of King Harold II of England, killed in the Battle of Hastings in 1066.

Surrey was divided into 14 hundreds, divisions of land somewhat similar to civil parishes today, each having a council which met to decide on community matters (see Hundred's Knoll in Chapter One). The origin of the word hundred is obscure, but it is usually assumed it defined an area of 100 hides, a hide being 120 acres which would support one family. Here it is used as a unit of rateable value, not of area.

The population of the county at the time of the Domesday Book has been calculated at 18,000.

The name Oxted

In the Domesday Book the name of the village is spelled 'Acstede', meaning 'place of oaktrees'. The 'x' is first recorded in 1202, 'Axsted', and in 1210-12 'Axstude', but it took a while longer before the 'O' crept in. In 1225 it was 'Ocsted', and by 1261 with 'Oxsted' it began to look recognisable to us today, but it didn't remain the same for ever after.

Standardised spelling is of course a recent phenomenon, and over the centuries the name has gone through every possible form, plus a few you might have thought impossible, like Hocstede or Okstide. It is a nice reminder of the name that some Oxted bus shelters are decorated with carved oak trees.

Oxted in the Domesday Book

The following is a translation of the section dealing with Oxted (see illustration):

> **LAND OF COUNT EUSTACE. IN TANDRIDGE HUNDRED.**
>
> Count Eustace holds Oxted. Gytha, Harold's mother, held it in the time of King Edward. Then it answered for 20 hides; now for 5 hides. Land for 20 ploughs. In lordship 2 ploughs; 34 villeins with 18 ploughs. 2 mills at 12s 6d; meadow, 4 acres; woodland, 100 pigs from pasturage; in Southwark, 1 dwelling at 2d; 6 serfs; 9 cottagers; a church, Value in the time of King Edward £16; when acquired £10; now £14.

Life in Oxted

The fortunes of the village varied over the years. The rateable area was 20 hides in the reign of King Edward, and now only five hides. (The abbreviation T.R.E. in the document means 'tempore regis Edwardi' - in the time of King Edward.) But the rateable value is now recovering from a low point reached 'when acquired', that is, in 1066. The point about the ploughs was that it was also a measure of the number of plough animals. The meadows of four acres would be water-meadows used for winter food for horses and oxen. The pigs would be let loose to forage in woodland.

So in medieval Oxted peasants were engaged in arable farming, with two mills to grind their corn and pigs being kept as well. Their spiritual needs were met by their own village church a short distance away. The population at the time was about 250 people.

In his book *Early Medieval Surrey*, John Blair says that Oxted was a typical example of the farming landscape of Wealden Surrey in that there was grazing on the downs in the north, enclosed fields belonging to the manor on the best land of the scarp slope, with a mixture of woodland, arable land and pasture on the southern two-thirds of the parish. Thus the long narrow shape of most of the parishes of Tandridge District reflects the necessity for different kinds of land to support the various needs of the population - they were fortunate to be able to spread across several different types.

Buildings

St Mary's Church

Building History: The mound on which the church stands is thought to have been a pre-Christian place of worship and burial ground. It was common for the first Christians to build on such sites, so as to consecrate them and to win over the non-Christians. The materials used in the church are mainly ironstone and sandstone.

Although there was a church here in Saxon times, the only signs left are at the bottom of the tower and some traces in the nave. About the middle of the 12C the tower, whose walls are five feet thick underground, was built (in two stages). About the same time parts of the nave walls and aisles were completed. The chancel is from the mid-13C. In the next two centuries, the 14C and 15C, the aisles were widened, the main walls were heightened using clunch, a chalky stone which comes from Godstone, and the chancel had new windows. The nave pillars and arches are again from the 15C. The church was damaged by fires in 1637 and 1716 so repair work was carried out then, and there was a major restoration in 1877 when attempts were made to restore the style more closely to the imagined medieval ideal. Thus a cupola shown on top of the tower on a lithographic plate of 1823 has been removed and crenellations added. The north aisle is also from this time.

The Church Today: As you approach the church you can see some of the evidence of building history in the changes in the stonework. You enter by the south porch where there is a sundial from 1815. The porch is 15C and the arms of the Cobham family, very battered, are on the small shields on the arch. Inside are the remains of a holy-water stoup and a plaque commemorating 900 years since the mention of the church in the Domesday Book. The great oak door is 14C, carved with foliage and with curious masks in the panels, very worn and hardly recognisable.

The 15C nave pillars are in Perpendicular style and you can still see embedded in the later pillars the remains of the earlier 13C or 14C arches which would have given a lower vault. At the end of the right-hand aisle there is a stairway cut into the pillar. This once led to the rood-loft which would have divided the nave from the chancel, where the oak screen (1903) is now. The wrought-iron chest in this aisle is probably 15C and from Flanders, and has an elaborate locking mechanism with twelve bolts on the inside of the lid but only one key. On the front of the chancel arch you can just see the faded remains of wall paintings, while above the arch is another plaque commemorating the 900th anniversary of the church.

St Mary's Church. The change of colour in the stonework shows where the walls were raised in the 14C

The iron chest in St Mary's

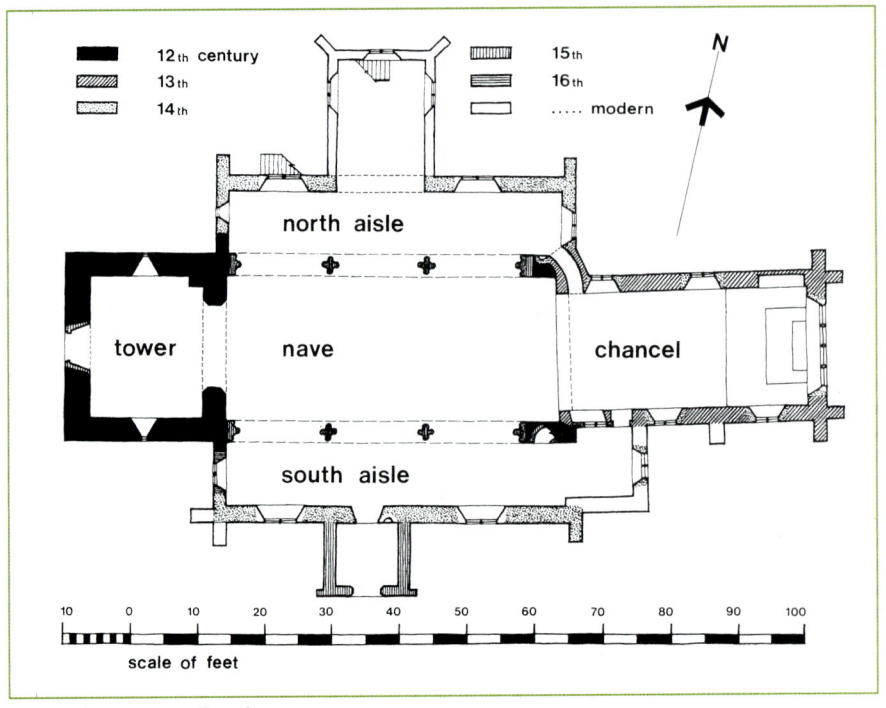

Plan of St Mary's Church

The long chancel (37ft) contains the oldest stained glass, now incorporated into the east window which has been considerably altered over the years. The 14C tracery has been mostly ground down, and the depictions of the evangelists, Matthew, Mark, Luke and John at the top are 14C stained glass fitted into a modern background.

The other two windows of the chancel are from the late 19C, the one on the north is a memorial to a member of the Hoskins family probably by the artist Charles Kempe while the other is by W.E. Tower who was Kempe's son-in-law. There is an arched niche in the wall which would have been used in the 13C for an Easter scene.

Back in the nave you can see the four large late 19C windows which are in the style of Burne-Jones and executed by the William Morris company, but after Morris's death. Three are in memory of other members of the Hoskins family.

At the back of the north aisle of 1877 stands the octagonal font from the 15C. Fonts were often eight-sided because the number eight was an ancient symbol for regeneration.

At the rear of the church there is another oak screen of 1931 through which you enter the ground floor of the tower where there are two 18C galleries with inscriptions detailing 17C and 18C charitable donations.

The church and the graveyard contain a very large number of memorials in the form of brasses, plaques, gravestones and tombs commemorating members of the Hoskins and Master families. An account of these with their inscriptions will be found in Chapters Three and Four dealing with the relevant period in which they lived.

Outside the south porch, the yew-tree is thought to be nearly 400 years old - venerable, but a mere baby compared to that of Tandridge nearby. The lych-gate commemorates the silver jubilee of George V in 1936. The cross on the mound is another Hoskins memorial, and besides the Hoskins graves, there are many other imposing chest tombs and vaults with grilles round them.

Over the centuries the churchyard has expanded into different sections, first the mound itself, then the adjoining part to the north and north-east (the 'new burial ground'). Across the lane is an extension, now virtually filled, and the further section at present in use is looked after by the Parish Council (i.e. the civil parish).

St Mary's and Master Park against the background of the North Downs

Manors of Oxted

Gradually over the centuries of the Middle Ages the large estates which had belonged to the Crown and great lords were broken into smaller units and came into the hands of lesser landowners. These 'landed gentry' became lords of the manor. Oxted eventually had five manors, Oxted, Birstead or Bursted, Broadham, Foyle and Stocketts. The first records we have of these manors are from the 13C or 14C.

Oxted Manor was Oxted Court Farm, situated opposite the south door of the church. Part of the manor in the reign of King John was held by Hugo de Nevill, and another part by Roland de Acstede, a local landowner who kept the old spelling of Oxted. He was clearly a man of distinction, for in 1290 he is recorded as being elected as one of the two Knights of the Shire (Surrey), equivalent to an MP. It is particularly interesting because he was one of the first such Knights.

For many years from 1344 Oxted manor together with its scattered lands belonged to the Cobhams who lived at Sterborough or Starborough Castle, now demolished, near Lingfield, and whose splendid tombs are in the church there. (The arms of Tandridge District Council contain stars which are a link with the Cobham arms.) The manor and farm would have been run for Lord Cobham by a steward who lived in the farm house. The house which in 1299 had consisted of a hall, a solar (upper room) and two other small rooms was repaired and new windows put in - but it was still not exactly palatial. Around this time the manor had 104 acres of oats and 64 acres of wheat which were the main crops, with some rye, barley and peas. Of course the demesne farm, that is, the farm of the manor itself, occupied the best land here on the south face of the North Downs and the peasants had to do certain work on it. There were 16 horses, 500 sheep and 90 cattle with pigs and goats as well. Workers were paid 8 shillings a year, and young servants received 4 shillings. The sheep were probably the only producers of actual profit beyond what was needed for subsistence.

In the 15C the manor came into the possession of the Burgh family, and in 1587 the first Charles Hoskins, 'citizen and merchant of London, did buy the manor and advowson of Oxted', which covered 605 acres, from a John Rede or Reade. By 1657, however, the Charles Hoskins of the time is described as of Barrow Green, so that Barrow Green Court had in effect become the manor house. The house called Court Farm at present on the site looks 19C, but behind the façade are structures from the 16C.

COURT FARM AND PARISH CHURCH, OXTED.

For centuries the demesne farm lay next to the church. This card was posted in 1908 and the wagon on the right belonged to Berry & Co., corn merchants of Oxted

Birsted Manor (or Biersted, Bursted) originally belonged to Tandridge Priory. In the 16C it belonged to a John Rede and it seems likely that he was the same John Rede who sold Oxted to Charles Hoskins. It too had many owners, and in the mid-19C it belonged to the Earl of Cottenham. The land holdings associated with this manor have not been identified.

Broadham Manor was not mentioned in the Domesday Book. The first mention of it was in the 14C as a possession of Battle Abbey. Mr W.J. Kilpatrick has published the history of the Manor of Broadham under the title *Broadham A Forgotten Manor* and these are mainly his findings. In the 14C the lands of the manor covered 217 acres. There was a manor house and enclosure, a mill, woods where pigs were kept, and lands described as arable, pasture, heath and meadow. Twenty-three tenants of different classes farmed 98 acres, and the rest of the land supported the manor.

The Reformation came and in 1538 the manor was granted with Limpsfield to Sir John Gresham of London the owner of Titsey Place. (More on the Gresham family will be found in Chapter Three.) Broadham continued in the Gresham family until the 18C. In 1719 it was sold to a John Blundell. In 1730 he fell out with William Hoskins lord of the manor of Oxted over payment of rents. After this the ownership of the manor passed from one distant relative to another, and various fractions of it were sold or otherwise acquired by different people. The title vanished in the early 20C. The house

St Mary's Church from the north-west

now named Broadham Manor is considered to represent the site of Broadham Farm, but there is no direct evidence that it was the site of the manor house itself.

Foyle Manor was for many years in the possession of the de Staffhurst family. In 1270 the rent was one clove gillyflower - a gillyflower was any kind of clove-scented flower such as a wallflower. (In similar vein, the rent for Rose Farm was one rose and a halfpenny.) The manor was sold in 1841 to William Leveson Gower of Titsey.

Stocketts Manor belonged to John atte Stockett in 1299 and remained in the same family for centuries. It was owned briefly by the Hoskins family. The present handsome house, L-shaped and brick built, is roofed with Horsham stone slates. The earliest part dates from the 15C and was refaced in the 17C. The east block is probably from 17C or 18C. Next to the house is the barn (17C), where concerts are held. (See Chapter Three.)

Watermills

Mills were vital for everyone's daily bread, and in the Middle Ages they would have belonged to the lord of the manor and the peasants had no alternative but to take their wheat there to be ground. Two mills are recorded in Domesday which were on the sites of **Oxted Upper Mill** and **Coltsford Mill**. (Oxted Upper Mill was situated behind what would become the site of the Wheatsheaf at the lower end of Old Oxted High Street.) However, by 1291 three were known to exist, and the third mill was on the site of the present **Oxted Mill**.

In John Senex's map of 1729 Coltsford Mill is called the Lower Mill, and Oxted Mill is called the Middle Mill. The Upper Mill must have ceased working by 1817 as some cottages were built on what had been the millpond by a man called John Cole.

Since the buildings of Coltsford are mainly from the 17C or 18C, and Oxted Mill is from the 19C, details will be found in Chapter Three and Chapter Four respectively.

Old Oxted

The village probably grew up in its present position because there was a crossing where the major route from Guildford to Canterbury met a track from London to Lingfield. Lingfield was relevant to Oxted because that was where the lord of Oxted Manor lived, and some of the scattered manor lands were in that area. The fact that the church and the manor house stood together nearly a mile away seems to have had little influence on the position of the settlement.

In the late Middle Ages the High Street was described as 'a great road which leads from the east to the west over the hill'. The hill has always been a problem, and the road level is much lower than the ground floor of the

The medieval crossroads with the Old Dairy (Lenton's Dairy)

houses, probably partly through wear and tear and partly because it was deliberately excavated. At one point an extra horse had to be kept at the bottom of the hill to help heavy wagons to the top.

The High Street, Brook Hill, part of the Godstone Road and part of Beadles Lane have been declared a Conservation Area. Most of the historic houses in Old Oxted were built late in the Middle Ages, when feudalism and serfdom had more or less died out. Peasants, craftsmen and farmers worked for themselves and enterprising merchants were setting up in business, so people were thinking of building their own comfortable and convenient homes. Each household had to be self-sufficient of course, and produce everything the family needed for daily life. Virtually nothing was produced to sell, except possibly wool.

In the late Middle Ages brick began to be used to fill the spaces between the timber framing, instead of clay and rubble. (It is a mystery why bricks fell into disuse in Britain for so many centuries after the Romans left. Bricks first reappeared in the 15C, then became common in the 16C.) About the same time the design of houses changed when it was found that a chimney on one wall was more convenient than a fire in the centre from which the smoke had to find its way out through a hole in the ceiling, choking the inhabitants as it went. Bricks helped here too, making chimneys easier to construct.

Three of the inns are buildings which were begun in medieval times. It seems that the **George Inn** was purpose-built for travellers' refreshment, probably in the late 15C. It was unusual in that it was built round a small courtyard, now filled in. Much was added and rebuilt especially in the 17C.

The Old Bell Inn did not start life as an inn. It must have been something quite grand because the first floor is taller than the ground floor, and Peter Gray suggests it might have been a guildhall or manorial court room, built perhaps in the late 15C, though much altered and extended since. In 1805 it was called the Five Bells.

The Crown Inn has a crosswing from about 1500, but the main part is early 18C. It has had a variety of names - in 1826 it was the Crown and Anchor, in 1906 the Crown Inn, in 1930 the Crown Hotel.

As for the dwellings, the typical medieval house was a 'hall house' - as its name implies, it consisted mainly of one large open hall where all activity took place and privacy was not an issue. It was only later that it became fashionable to have lots of smaller rooms dedicated to different purposes such as eating, sleeping, working or receiving visitors. The hall was floored across at half height, often over half its area, and later might be completely

The George Inn

The Old Bell, situated on the medieval crossroads

The Crown Inn

floored over, which would give double the amount of original living space. Hall houses continued to be built into the first half of the 16C and are thus still considered 'medieval'. Many Oxted houses come into this category.

The earliest dwelling still remaining on the High Street is **Crown Hill Cottages**, a group of four that once formed a capacious hall house of the early 14C. In the 17C a floor was inserted to increase the area available. When the roof was investigated it was found that a layer of oak twigs complete with acorns had been used for insulation. The brick front was probably added in the 18C. Nos. 14 and 16 were rebuilt in the 16/17C, but no. 18 retains all the original timber work, with massive beams and braces.

On the same side of the road, **Oak** and **Beam Cottages** were another 15C hall house with the present façade dating from around 1900. They were joined about the late 18C to **Forge Cottage**, which had a forge in the garden behind.

On the crossroads opposite the Old Bell stands the house known as **The Old Dairy**, which is joined to the next-door cottages. The owner Mr Butcher has kindly supplied the survey done in 1971 when it was found that part of the building was from the early 15C with an open hall. Next came the part which stands forward of the rest on the road and the central part was rebuilt in the 16C. It appears that it was business premises, as it occupied such a prominent position on the junction of the roads.

On the other side of the road, **Bennetts Cottage** and the **Old Lock-up** have a complicated building history. It started with Bennetts which was a late 1480s hall-type farmhouse about two-thirds as wide as the present house, built end-on to the road because of the steep slope. The solar was at the street end and the service area at the other end. In the 17C a wing was constructed across the end on the street side, which was the width of the present house. Then in the 19C the resulting L-shape was filled in. The wing became known as the Old Lock-up when it was used as the workhouse in the 19C and the cellar was put into use as a gaol. The house has retained the original timbers, some with old carpenters' marks, and a crown-post in the attic. The owners found that on removing a Victorian fireplace they had a splendid inglenook behind. The Old Lock-up itself is partly below ground level and about the size of a garage with one small high window.

Forge, Oak and Beam Cottages

Bennetts and Old Lockup

Going up the hill on the same side, the cottages now called **Terrace** and **Huddle** formed two hall houses of the 15C with the very high gabled addition **Streeters** being put in as a new wing in the 16C. The small war memorial on the wall of Huddle Cottage led to it being once called Shrine Cottage.

Old Town House and **Catmint Cottage** formed part of a hall house of late medieval times, that is, the early 16C. The **Old Bank House** was originally a hall house of the late 15C, later floored over and converted to two storeys, now with 19C shop fronts. Round the corner in Beadles Lane **Old Cottage** extends behind London House. It was a hall house of the late 15C.

In Brook Hill, **Brook House** was first built in the 16C, as a very shallow building from front to back, with jettied (overhanging) upper storey both front and back which was unusual. It might thus have been something other than a house, and possibly on an 'island'. In the 17C it was extended and the jetties filled in to give extra space downstairs.

Barrow Green Farm was originally built as a hall house facing Hogtrough Lane which was the route from Oxted to London. The present building is thought to be a wing added on to this house and may have been the home of the Hoskins family before they built Barrow Green Court.

At **Hurst Green, Sheppards Barn** was not named after a shepherd neither was it a barn, so it is a complete misnomer. It seems that a John Shepherde was a tithe collector in Broadham in 1417, so he may have been the builder. It too was a hall house, as was **Old Meldrum** across the green. Here, as was usual, a floor was afterwards inserted to give two storeys but this subsequently proved too low for comfort. So a drastic step was taken at some stage in its history when the house was completely dismantled and rebuilt with a higher ground floor. An extension was added in the 19C.

Old Cottage and **Mayflower Cottage** face each other across **Broadham Green**, both revealing the crooked old beams framing brick infill, with just one or two panels of whitewash to add to the picturesque appearance.

At **Merle Common** there is **Merle Common House**, again a picturesque building of the early 16C, but with much renovation and extension. **Jincox** or **Gincocks Farm** is of about the same date, with tile-hung façade. The main hall was floored over later the same century.

Mayflower Cottage at Broadham Green

Medieval Tandridge

Tandridge Priory was just over the present Oxted/Tandridge parish boundary on Barrow Green Road. This was founded in about 1200 for the Augustinians, but nothing now remains except the fishponds, a necessary source of food. Previously there had been here a Hospital of St James, to cater for the needs of travellers, the poor and the sick. The priory was dissolved by Henry VIII at the Reformation. Now the name belongs to a 17C listed building. The seal of the priory contained three gold circles which are now incorporated into the arms of Tandridge District Council. **St Peter's Church** is even older than the priory, with some parts dating from 1100, but the most impressive features are the oak beams of the bell-tower and the roof timbers of the nave and chancel. Outside is the gigantic yew, said by some to be 2000 years old.

Medieval Limpsfield

St Peter's Church was founded in Norman times and had a major renovation in the 13C. Many famous musicians are buried in the graveyard - see Chapter Five. Limpsfield was an important part of the lands of Battle Abbey and the Abbot held a court here in the house now known as **Old Court Cottage**, Titsey Road, one of the oldest domestic timber buildings in southern England, if not the oldest. This was built about 1190 or 1200 by Bishop Odo of Battle, who had been Prior of St Augustine's in Canterbury, thus a very important prelate. Almost every house in picturesque **Limpsfield High Street** has a long history.

By the end of the Middle Ages Oxted was a thriving town on a busy road, with many prestigious hall houses for independent merchants, while out in the countryside were commodious farmhouses for the farmers whose products were the lifeblood of the town and who now could work for themselves and not for the lord of the manor.

Chapter Three

Early Modern Times 16C-18C

The three centuries after the Renaissance and Reformation were a time of growth and consolidation. The number of sturdy farmhouses increased rapidly, and more businesses began to take root as the merchant class became larger and more self-confident. The steep High Street became a compact town clustered on the crossroads and along the highway, assured of passing trade as traffic flowed from Guildford to Canterbury and back.

How the Town Grew

To all intents and purposes, in Oxted the Middle Ages lasted until the middle of the 16C as regards style in village houses and farmhouses, with hall houses still the main type. In the village itself there was not much room left along the main street. One building of consequence of the 16C was **Oxted Court** near the church, the site of the manor farm of the Middle Ages (see Chapter Two). However, it has been renovated so many times that it no longer looks old.

Chimneys which in the 15C had begun to be attached to an outside wall instead of in the middle of the room assumed greater significance, with elegant fireplaces to burn the coal which was becoming more common as fuel. In fact, by the end of the 16C houses were becoming very civilised indeed, with carpets, pictures and decorated ceilings.

It should be remembered of course that the buildings which remain today are not the only ones that existed - only the survivors.

Seventeenth Century

This was a century of more ambitious building, especially towards the later years. It was a prosperous time for Surrey which rose from being the 18th richest county in 1636 to the second richest county in 1693. (Middlesex was the richest, because it encompassed much of London.)

In 1680 **John Seller** published a map which marks 'Okested' and 'Okested Place', and alongside are 'Limsfield' and 'Limsfield More House' with a little clump of trees drawn just above, dividing them from 'Titesley'. This is a good example of the variations in spelling over time, since in the previous century Saxton's map of 1575 spells Oxted as we do today though Limpsfield is 'Lymsfelde'.

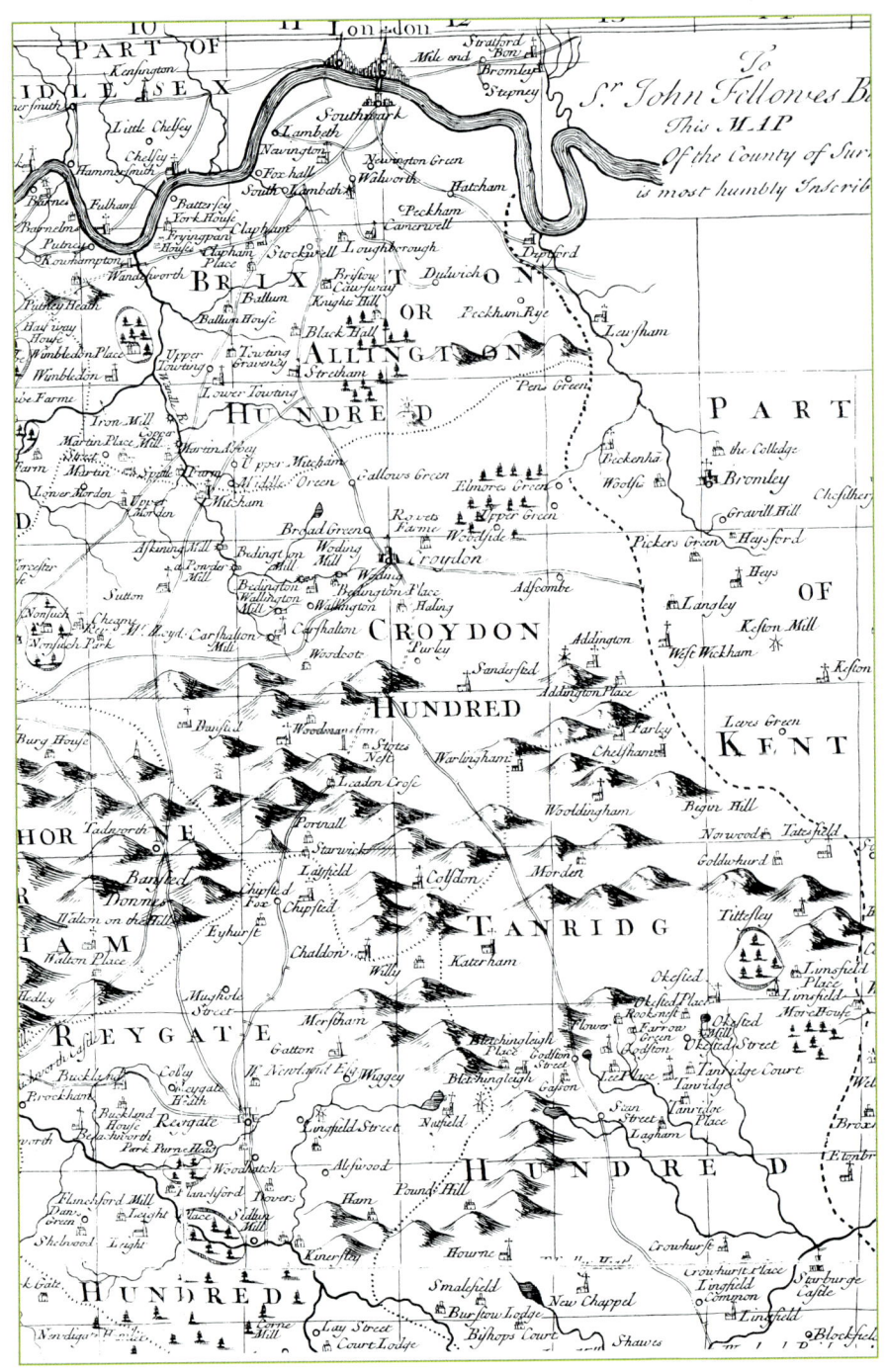

John Seller's map of 1680

Now was a time of change in the building trade. The picturesque hall houses were no longer being built, and brick was beginning to be popular. There was a need for a different type of home, that is to say, humbler houses in the village, or grand country mansions, or comfortable farmhouses. On the High Street there was just room for **Flaxman Cottages** and **The Nest**, and the timber-framed building behind the old Post Office is of about the same age, though the Post Office itself and the two cottages next to it were built very much later, probably in the early 19C. Originally a barn as the name implies, **Old Barn Cottage**, tucked away off the High Street, could be from the 17C or 18C, with an extension in the 19C. **Beadles Cottage** round the corner in Beadles Lane is actually the 17C extension of an earlier house.

Further south, **Harling Cottages** in Tanhouse Road next to The Haycutter were first built as one house, which in about 1700 was extended to the west.

Further out again, large farmhouses began to be constructed, such as **Sunt Farmhouse**. The barn of Sunt Farm was built probably late in the 17C, but has been recently converted into a house. **Perrysfield farmhouse**, a large L-shaped building, was begun. The barn nearby is from roughly the same date, as is **Stocketts Manor barn**. Here the roof beams, gallery and cavernous fireplace now make it an atmospheric concert hall. It once stood on the north-west side of

The Nest and Flaxman Cottages

the house, but was moved to the south-west and reconstructed for use as a ballroom. Presumably this is when the fireplace was added as it seems an unlikely luxury for the inhabitants of a barn. (See Chapter Two for Stocketts Manor itself.)

The grandest house, **Barrow Green Court**, was built in the early 17C and much of it is still of this period, though remodelled. (Grade I listed.) It is of three storeys including the dormer windows, of red brick, with handsome bay windows, and originally based on a typical E-shape without the central bar, though the space has since been somewhat filled by extensions and alterations in the 18C and 19C. The style is mainly Jacobean with a Georgian façade and it has very fine Jacobean panelled rooms, with stately fireplaces and one particularly good ceiling of moulded plasterwork. The library is in Regency style and has bookcases with brass grilles.

The estate came into the possession of a Charles Hoskins in 1657 and came to be regarded as the manor house of Oxted in place of Oxted Court near St Mary's church. Its owners were thus the lords of the manor, while Oxted Court became purely a farm. In 1768 another Charles Hoskins died without a male heir and the manor passed through marriage to the Master family. The Masters however included the name Hoskins in their name so that there is a certain continuity. However, other owners or tenants are recorded, including Jeremy Bentham the 18/19C author and reformer, and George Grote the 19C historian. Before World War I the Hoskins Masters let it to a William McGrath. Then the family appear to have left, and in 1931 it is described as returning to the Master family when Captain C.E.H. Master came to live there. He died in 1960. Later in the 1960s it was owned by Christopher Rowley who repaired and refurbished it and opened it to the public. (Admission 5s.) It now belongs to Mohamed al Fahed the owner of House of Fraser, a business empire which includes Harrods. His son Dodi, who died in the car crash which killed Princess Diana, is buried in the grounds. The estate has stables for the handsome Harrods' Friesian horses which can be seen on public occasions in Oxted drawing immaculate green and gold Harrods' vehicles driven by top-hatted coachmen.

The Hoskins Family

During this period city merchants began to purchase land to build impressive country houses and assumed the position of lords of the manor. The Oxted manor was held by the Hoskins family, and later the Masters, while at Titsey a very illustrious family, the Greshams, came to live, followed by the Leveson Gowers.

It has been noted previously that the earliest reference to a Hoskins in Oxted comes in 1587 when 'Charles Hoskins, citizen and merchant of London, did buy the manor and advowson of Oxted' from one John Rede or Reade. Hoskins is described as coming from Monmouthshire. For over 200 years the Hoskins family were the lords of the manor of Oxted and from their mansion Barrow Green Court they wielded power and influence over every aspect of life in the town.

Then the succession ran out. William Hoskins who died in 1762 was succeeded by his son Charles, whose daughter married three husbands one after the other. On her death the property passed to her aunt, Katherine Master. Her son was the Rev Lech (or Legh) Hoskins Master, and his son was named Charles Lech Hoskins Master. (Further history of the Masters will be found in Chapter Four.)

The arms of the Hoskins family consist of a shield with three lions and a chevron, with a crest of a cock's head.

The most accessible records of the family are in the memorials and tombs in St Mary's Church where they were baptised, worshipped, and were finally buried and commemorated in stone or brass, on the walls or in the floor. The following table summarises the main information to be gathered from the church about the family during the 17C and 18C.

Hoskins memorials in St Mary's

1611	Thomas Hoskins	age 5, son of Thomas Hoskins
1611	Thomas	age 6 months, son of Thomas Hoskins
1613	John Hoskins	age 5, fourth son of Thomas Hoskins
1651	wife of	Charles Hoskins, daughter of William Hale, age 42
1657	Charles Hoskins	son of Sir Thomas Hoskins, age 54
1676	Edmund Hoskins	second son of Charles Hoskins born 1634
1702	Dame Ann Hoskins	
1712	Sir William Hoskins	of Oxted, Knight, aged 83. Elder son of Charles Hoskins
1712	George Bond	age 46. Married the daughter of Charles Hoskins
1717	John Hoskins	(tomb in graveyard)
1728	Elizabeth Bond	second daughter of Charles Hoskins, age 82 mother of George Bond.
1755	Charles Hoskins	age 85
1776	Rachel	wife of above age 73

The brass to five-year-old Thomas and his 6-month-old brother, also Thomas, has two figures of children in long gowns of which the head is missing from the larger - these look like girls not boys. The text runs:

> HERE LYETH ENTERRED THE BODY OF THOMAS HOSKINS, GENT: SECOND SONNE OF S[R] THOMAS HOSKINS KNIGHT WHO DECEASED Y[E] 10TH DAY OF APRILL A[O] DNO . 1611. ATT Y[E] AGE OF 5 YEARES: WHO ABOVTE A QUARTER OF AN HOVRE BEFORE HIS DEPTURE DID OF HIMSELFE W[TH] OVT ANY INSTRUCTION, SPEAKE THOS WORDES: & LEADE VS NOT INTO TEMPTATIO, BVT DELIVER US FROM ALL EVILL, BEINGE Y[E] LAST WORDS HE SPAKE: HERE ALSO LYETH ENTERRED Y[E] BODY OF THOMAS HOSKINS GENT THE FIFTE SONNE OF S[R] THOMAS HOSKINS KNIGHT, WHO DECEASED THE 13TH OF MARCH A[O] 1611 BEINGE HALFE A YEARE OF AGE

Yet another son of these unhappy parents died two years later. The brass to John, aged five, shows a young boy wearing a short cloak, and the text reads:

> HERE LYETH INTERRED THE BODY OF IOHN HOSKINS THE FOVRTH SONNE OF S[R] THOMAS HOSKINS KNIGHT WHO DYED THE XIXTH DAY OF IVLY A[O] DNI 1613 BEINGE OF Y[E] AGE OF V YERES

All these three were sons of Sir Thomas Hoskins and his wife Dorothy who was the daughter of John Aldersey mentioned below.

The slab to the left of the south door well away from other family graves is evidently the result of some deep family rift. Aged only 42, **Edmund Hoskins** died in 1676:

> Hic jacet EDMUNDUS HOSKINS, filius secundo-genitus Caroli Hoskins de Oxted in Comit. Surriae, armigieri; natus est XII° Februar. an'o salutis MDCXXXIIII°, mortuus X° denatus XII° Junii MDCLXXVI° . Non sine ingento animi mœrore sensit se ab irato patre quasi exhæredatum; noluit igitur inter familiæ cineres sepeliri sed hunc semotum requiescendi elegit locum. M. H. charissimo conjugi mœstissima conjux. F.C.

(A partial translation is as follows: Here lies Edmund Hoskins second son of Charles Hoskins of Oxted in the County of Surrey, knight; born 12th February in the year of salvation 1634, died 10th June 1676. ...... he felt as if disinherited by his irate father; he did not wish therefore to be buried among the family ashes but he chose to rest in this remote place.)

Two long-suffering Hoskins ladies are commemorated in verse: one who died in 1651 has this memorial:

> Let this
>
> Patterne of Piety
>
> Mapp of Misery
>
> Mirrour of Patience
>
> Here Rest

Dame Ann Hoskins died in 1702 and is remembered in this verse:

> Let those in after ages know
>
> This Vertuous woman here below
>
> Was stable in religion pious in life
>
> A charitable creature an humble wife
>
> In her affliction dolorous and many
>
> Her patience scarcely paralleled by any
>
> Of perfect happiness she could not miss
>
> Led by such graces to Eternal bliss

In the chancel is the imposing stone carved memorial of **John Aldersey** with his wife and all seventeen of their children, two of whom married into the Hoskins family. They are represented kneeling under an arch with a shield above, and at the sides are the arms of the Haberdashers and the Merchant Adventurers. The inscription reads:

> JOHN ALDERSEY, haberdasher and merchant venturor of London, being son of John Aldersey of Bunbery in ye County of Chester, gent. dep. y^s lyfe ye 26 day of July a^o 1616, being of the age of 75 years, and having lived with his wth Anna in the holy Æstate of matrimony 46 years, and had issue 17 children.

The oldest brass is from 1428 and is that of a rector of the parish, John Page (name unclear). Rector Ralph Rand who died in 1648 is rather easier to understand. His wife Mary died aged 72 in 1638, and his wife Joan died aged 64 in 1641. Rand was rector of Oxted from 1615 to 1648, previously rector of Gatton, and died aged 88 - which means he must have married for the second time at about 80 years of age a lady well over 60.

A large memorial is to William Finch in 1728, and his wife who is called a spinster. Attached to the same plaque is the mention of Charles Hoskins (1755)

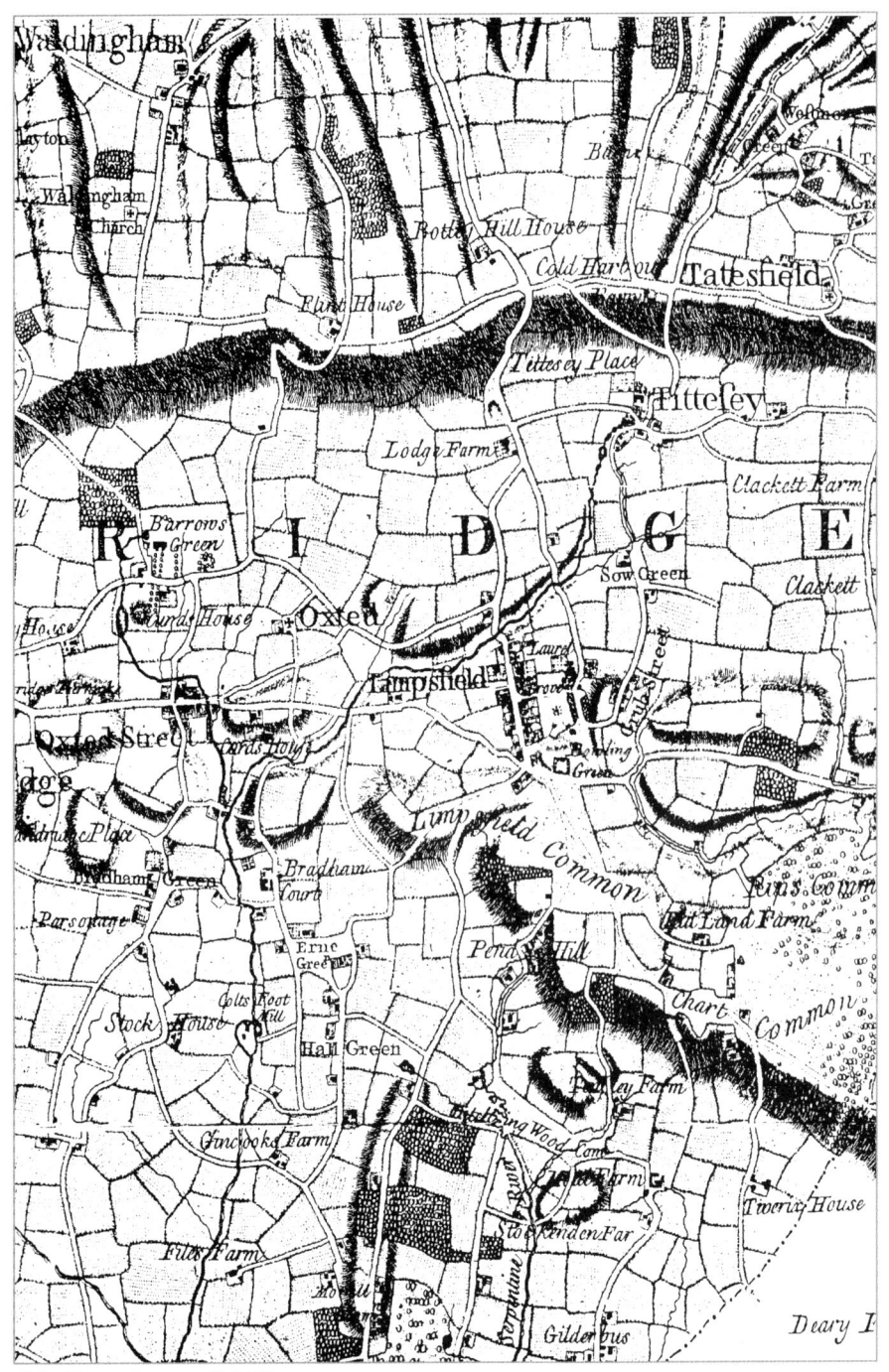

John Rocque's map of 1762

and his wife Rachel (1776). In the floor there is a stone slab to the wife of Charles Hoskins 1651, and Charles himself, son of Sir Thomas, 1657. The prettiest brass is that of Johanne Haselden (1480) wearing a charming dress trimmed with fur and graceful draped head-dress. In the nave floor are grave-slabs to John Hoskins and his wife, 1712, and Sir William Hoskins, 1712.

In the churchyard behind the east end of the church there is a large tomb of John Hoskins who died in 1717 aged 77.

EIGHTEENTH CENTURY

In 1718 **John Aubrey** published *The Natural History and Antiquities of Surrey*. This consists of a brief summary of each parish followed by a description of the church. His portrayal of Oxted is as follows:

> **OXSTED,** *call'd* **Ocksted,** *and* **Okestede,**
>
> Is in the Deanery of Ewell, in the Parish of *Stoke-Dabernon* and lies very low. It was in the Time of King *Edw.I.* in the Possession of *Reginald*, Lord *Cobbam* of *Stereborough*, who follow'd that brave Prince in his Expedition into *France*, was his Embassador to *Rome*, was in the Vantguard under the Conduct of the *Black Prince* at *Cressy* and *Poictiers*, where the *English* Nation obtain'd immortal Honour, and died of the Plague, *Octob, 5.* 1360; by his Demise it came to his Wife *Joane*, Daughter of *Maurice de Berkeley*, who died *Octob. 2.* 1369, seiz'd of the Manour, and left it to her son *Reginald*, who departed this Life, *6 July 1402*. The Church, with a handsom Spire, lies at some small Distance from the Town, and is in the Patronage of the Family of *Hoskins's*, who are also Lords of this Manour.

It is noticeable that the greater proportion of the piece is devoted to Lord Cobham (who did not even live here), but he mentions the Hoskins's briefly, and also the church, which at that time had a spire.

John Rocque's map of 1762 shows the road from Godstone following Church Lane and Station Road West, then going over the site of the station and down Amy Road to Bluehouse Lane. The latter end of Amy Road fell into disuse, became a sort of bog and is now part of the car-park.

The 18C was the time of the agricultural revolution with huge advances in growing crops and breeding stock, so that animals could be kept over winter instead of being slaughtered in autumn. Small farms were enclosed to make large holdings so that farmers became rich and labourers poor. Improved

The Pound in Sandy Lane

roads meant that these disenchanted labourers could move more easily to the towns. Thus more small cottages as well as large mansions were built, but not so many medium size dwellings for the middle classes.

In the **High Street**, there was not much room for further building, but many houses were extended or remodelled at this time, for example, Oak, Beam, and Forge Cottages, Bennetts and the Old Lock-up, Crown Hill Cottages and the George. **The White House** on the Godstone Road was constructed in the 18C but the windows and the white rendering were added in the 19C. The tiny timber house, **Low Cottage**, at the bottom of the hill was probably completed about this time too, but its handsome stone extension, the Stone House, was added only in the 19C to join two little cottages. Space must have been getting tight in the 18C, because several new developments spread up Beadles Lane - **Hillview** and its companion, and **Standwell House**, as well as the cottages **Yew Tree, Orchard** and **Rose**. With all this expansion, there seems to have been trouble with stray animals, for the **pound** was constructed in Sandy Lane, on the roadside just beyond the bend.

A little further away, **Hall Hill** at Broadham Green was built and later extended, and **Holly Cottage, Merle Common Cottages** and **Comforts Farm Cottage** were also constructed in this century.

Although **Hurst Green** did not really expand until the railway came, several large attractive houses were built around the green centuries before. The first mention of the area seems to have been in 1577 as Herste Grene. The meaning of the name is 'Wood Green'. On Rocque's map it appears as Erne Green, obviously a name misheard by the compilers. Here three buildings are shown, which from their positions must be Sheppards Barn with Forge Cottage, Home Farm and Old Meldrum. (For Sheppards Barn and Old Meldrum see Chapter Two. The present Forge Cottage is a later house on the site of a former forge.)

On the same map, south of 'Erne Green' is Hall Green, a name which later developed into '**Holland**' ('Hall Land'), thus nothing to do with the Netherlands, as one might think.

Between later houses on the green stands **Home Farm**, which was never actually a farm, though the land was taken from Tanhouse Farm. It was originally constructed about 1750, and considerably enlarged in the 19C. The owner Dr Bowyer has researched the history of the house, and points out that it would be too grand for a farmer of those times, having two fair-sized rooms, one either side of the hall. Instead it had several different uses over its long history including the possibility that it was a pub called the Jolly Sailor. (The 1841 census mentions such a pub and there doesn't seem to be any other candidate for the position.) Then in 1894 it belonged to a bailiff

Rose, Orchard and Yew Tree Cottages

called George Knight, and the road on which it stands was then called Knight's Hill. In 1920 it was put up for rent at the princely sum of £60 per year, and in 1952 it was sold for £4950. Now it retains original beams, and a handsome inglenook fireplace with hooks for food and inbuilt salt cupboard. The garden is bounded by the River Eden, which is crossed by the steeply humped and very picturesque stone-built **Packhorse Bridge**. The bridge can hardly have had anything to do with packhorses since it is not on a track or path, and appears simply to have linked the fields of Tanhouse Farm. The date of its construction is uncertain - all that can be said is that it is post-medieval.

In this century too there was built another imposing house in the neighbouring parish of Titsey, and the family who lived there included among their members some who played a part on the international stage in the Elizabethan era.

Titsey Place has the postal address of Oxted but is in the ancient parish of Titsey. The history of the house and the families who lived there are important because of the national and international significance of the Greshams in the 16C. Later, the family were linked to the Hoskins's by marriage and played a leading role in local life and society. The mansion is open to visitors in the summer.

Titsey Place

There was a house on this site for hundreds of years, but what we can recognise today was built mainly in 1775, that is, the two-storey section. The previous dwelling was first demolished and Sir John Gresham had the new house built in red brick. He also moved the church and village to their present positions because he considered that they were too near the house. All this work was partly financed by Hoskins money, inherited from his uncle. It was faced with 'Roman cement' in 1826. The rest of the house, the three-storey tower-like portion, was added in 1856.

There are three shields over the entrance - the one on the porch contains the crest of the Greshams, the grasshopper, above the window is the coat of arms of the Greshams, and on the parapet is the Leveson Gower coat of arms.

Inside, much of the house remains as it was refurbished to designs of William Atkinson in 1826. The entrance hall has several distinguished family portraits, including some by Lely, Romney and Thomas Lawrence.

The rooms are shown to the public in the following order. The library has a portrait of Sir Thomas Gresham by Antonio More between the bookcases fashioned from oak grown on the estate. There are four Canaletto paintings, commissioned by one of the Hoskins family while the painter was living in England in the mid 18C.

The dining-room is in the Regency style and has good furniture and porcelain. The staircase with cast-iron balustrade leads to the landing with two Boule cabinets. The sitting-room has panels from the 16C, 17C and 18C and a bow-window with a view of the garden. The gallery bedroom is decorated in yellow with a pedimented fireplace.

Downstairs again, the beamed and panelled Old Hall was the servants' hall, and has a large fireplace cavity with a built-in spice cupboard. Here there are displays of christening clothes, and finds from the Roman villa excavated in the grounds.

The 'old' dining room is in the new tower added to the building in 1856 and has dark Victorian panelling and decoration. It has a portrait of two of the last owners and their dogs.

The décor in the drawing-room was altered in the 1920s to lighter pastel colours, and contains porcelain by Derby, Worcester and Meissen.

In the **Grounds**, you can see lining the drive some of the remaining Wellingtonia trees planted by Granville Leveson Gower to celebrate his 16 children. The formal garden is terraced with steps and wide herbaceous borders, with clipped box spirals along the top terrace nearest the house and a tributary of the Eden forming a pretty feature with a fountain and bridges. The rose garden surrounds a circular lawn and beside it is the yew, said to be 1000 years old, which is where the church once stood. Dogs are buried alongside.

The extensive estate includes the 210-acre beech plantation and the scant remains of the **Roman villa** of which almost nothing is now visible. This was excavated in the 1864, and measured 130ft. by 55ft., with two long corridors linking the rooms. There was a hypocaust at one end to heat the house, and it appears to have been occupied in the second century AD. Later it seems to have been adapted as an industrial site, as evidence of fulling was discovered. (Fullers' earth, a type of calcium used in the preparation of cloth, can be found not far away at Nutfield.) Some of the finds from the excavations are shown in the house.

The Greshams and Leveson Gowers

In the 16C the manor of Titsey was bought by Sir John Gresham, a prosperous and influential London merchant, whose family originally hailed from Norfolk. Sir John and his brother Sir Richard each became Lord Mayor of London. They were leaders in the world trade of the time and travelled far and wide, even to Russia, in search of exotic goods. In 1537 they were each granted the privilege of a crest on their coats of arms, and each chose a grasshopper, supposedly because of the similarity of the name with 'Gresham'.

Richard's son, Sir Thomas Gresham, eventually became even more powerful. He advised and served all the Tudor monarchs from Henry VIII to Elizabeth on national financial affairs and was a Crown agent, ambassador and chancellor, but his proudest and most celebrated achievement was the building of the first Royal Exchange in 1566.

Thomas' uncle, Sir John, acquired Titsey and several other manors in Surrey and surrounding counties in 1534. It was said he could ride to London from Titsey without leaving his own land. Greshams continued at Titsey with varying fortunes through the years.

 In 1724 Sir Marmaduke married Ann Hoskins thus linking Titsey with the old Oxted family. Unfortunately the name was set to die out, for at the beginning of the 19C Katharine Maria Gresham was the last of the name. In 1804 she married William Leveson Gower, a relative of the Duke of Sutherland, and thus the Leveson Gowers came to Titsey.

It was Granville William Leveson Gower who made the most radical impression on the estate and house in the 19C. He was deeply interested in history and genealogy, and many of the antiquarian additions to the house are his, such as the coats of arms. He rebuilt and renamed St James's Church, since it is on the old Pilgrims' Way which exits from Titsey Park at that point, and St James is the patron saint of pilgrims.

Finally in the 20C the family dwindled to four bachelor brothers, who in their care for the estate formed the Titsey Foundation to preserve the house and gardens for the public. The last Leveson Gower of Titsey died in 1992.

The Gresham crest of a grasshopper continues to link this part of the world with the present Royal Exchange, where the grasshopper sits on the weather-vane, and Tandridge District Council's coat of arms is surmounted by a green grasshopper.

The names of Gresham Road and Granville Road in Limpsfield perpetuate the memory of the family.

Watermills

In 1086 when the Domesday Book was compiled there were around 120 watermills in Surrey. Usually the stream they used for power was not strong enough to turn the wheels without extra help, so the usual method was for the stream to be dammed by a sluice-gate at night and the resulting full mill-pond to be used for driving the mill during the day. Most Surrey mills

Coltsfold Mill

used 'overshot' wheels. That is to say, the stream of water hit the wheel on the top edge so that the weight of the water in the attached buckets was heavy enough to turn the wheel. The grain had to be lifted high enough to feed the millstones from above, and this could be done either from a built-out part of an upper storey (a luccam or lucomb) or through a trap-door. The millstone might be of either Derby Peak (Millstone Grit) for grinding coarse cattle-food, or French Burr Stone which produced finer-grained flour.

There were two mills mentioned in Domesday Book for Oxted. (See Chapter Two.) **Coltsford Mill** was built in the 17C or 18C, but there has been a mill on the site at least since the date of the Domesday Book. On John Rocque's map of 1762 it is called Colts Foot. It is brick, with weatherboarding above, and has a very long steep mansard roof. It stands picturesquely beside the mill-pond, now developed as a fishery. In 1866 it was bought by a miller named William Heasman, possibly the William Heasman who owned Oxted Mill or perhaps his son. He was evidently an enterprising and modern-minded man, for he installed a new overshot external wheel of 16ft. in diameter by about 4ft. across, as well as other new machinery. However, as it is downstream of the Oxted Mill, there was some inconvenience when the roller mill there began working as it needed six times as much water as the old type. Thus it ran out of water from the mill-pond sooner and so the miller closed the sluice-gates to store water for the next day, and left the stream short of water in the lower reaches. Here there are five pairs of millstones, three French Burr and two Derby Peak. The mill-pond has an unusual overflow system, consisting of a 10ft. diameter brick basin set in the floor of the pond so that excess water drains over its edge.

It stopped commercial grinding in 1940 because of grain shortages in World War II, but was for some years occasionally set in motion again and was claimed to be the last working mill in Surrey. The whitewashed and beamed ground level storage area is now used as a restaurant. Here you can glimpse a part of the machinery, and the sacking chutes in the ceiling used to channel the flour down from the floor above.

By the end of the 18C, society had changed. The families in the manors took on the role of the ruling lords of the Middle Ages, and they built themselves imposing mansions as befitted their status and wealth. Homes were much more comfortable and people had more choice in the way they lived. But even greater changes lay ahead, with the industrial revolution and the mechanisation of almost every aspect of life.

Chapter Four

The Nineteenth Century

This is the century in which germinated the seeds of modern life as we know it. In Oxted the industrial revolution did not occasion large factory or mining developments because the prerequisite raw materials were not available. But it was one of the results of the industrial revolution, the railway, which caused the greatest upheaval in our local history.

Before the Railway

Oxted was not exactly important at the beginning of the 19C. In fact, there is one map of Surrey from 1815 on which it is not even marked. But the population, which in Domesday times was 250, more than doubled in the course of the 19C. It was 644 in 1801, then it was 1064 half-way through the century in 1851, and by 1891 it was 1499.

In the first half of the 19C, Pigot and Co.'s Directory for 1839 gives the following description:

> Adjoining to the parish of Limpsfield is that of OXTED, in the same hundred; the village, a neat little rural place, is about three miles N.E. from Godstone. The country in this neighbourhood is in a fine state of cultivation, abounding with wood and water, and containing many respectable residences. The church, standing nearly a mile from the village, is of Gothic architecture, but possessing no feature of particular interest. The benefice is a rectory, in the gift of the family of Masters. A fair is held here on the 1st May. The inhabitants of this parish are chiefly employed in agriculture, and their number, by the last census, was 959.

The same directory gives lists of the gentry and clergy, schools and various tradespeople. Oxted had two schools, two bakers, two butchers, two blacksmiths and four boot and shoe makers. What is surprising is the number of women engaging in trades traditionally thought of as the province of men only. Judith Lashmar is named as both a brewer and maltster (Lashmar's Brewery was on the site of the block of flats variously known as the Brewery or Brew House Flats on the High Street). Even more unusual in our eyes is that Mary Worsell was a bricklayer and Mary Bray was a carpenter. Richard Bray was a wheelwright and one can imagine a

Oxted Mill

husband-and-wife team here. (Limpsfield, not to be outdone in equal opportunities, had a lady wheelwright.) There were also two 'Grocers, Drapers and Dealers in Sundries', two millers, one painter/plumber, one saddler and one tailor. Three inns are mentioned, the Bell, the Crown & Anchor and the George, but not the Wheatsheaf.

However, if in 1839 you needed a watchmaker, a hairdresser, a gardener, a corn dealer or to catch a coach to London or elsewhere, you had to go to Godstone or Limpsfield. This list of businesses shows that households depended on shops for their daily needs and no longer produced everything for themselves. Thus the idea began to spread that shops might stock items which could only be obtained from a distance, whether in England or abroad so that exotic foods and furnishings were not just for the upper classes.

Building Development

In the early part of the 19C there was some new building in the village, and it is clear that it was designed for humbler citizens. The seven cottages of **Shorters Row** had one room on each floor, and since they are built into the side of the hill there is no window at the back of the ground floor. The builder was John Shorter and he put these up between 1839 and 1856. The two brick cottages adjoining were added some time before 1870. **Barn** and

Dairy Cottages on Godstone Road were originally a barn but are recorded in 1814 as two wooden cottages.

As mentioned previously, the Stone House was added to the tiny Low Cottage in the 19C. Nos. 1-3 Godstone Road with their distinctive round-headed windows were built on the site of a previous medieval house and were for many years antique shops. The **Old Post Office**, **Frazers** and **Saddlers Cottages** were built at this time too, with the Post Office adjoining the earlier wing at the back. Frazers was a bakery, complete with a stone oven, while Saddlers was a harness-maker's until the1960s. A house on the site of **Berrys Cottage** and **Newton** is recorded in the 18C, but the present cottages came into being only in the 19C.

On West Hill, then called Cottage Hill, **Oxted Cottage**, now **West Hill House**, was built in a neo-Gothic style. In the first part of the 19C it was owned by the Bellis family with Lt. Colonel Bellis registered as the owner in 1832. He and some of his family are buried in St Mary's churchyard. The house was enlarged to its present size probably in the middle of the century

Shorters Row

Beadles Lane School of 1872. The block on the right was the head teacher's house

by the Walker family, which is not surprising as one owner had eight children (and nine more children by a second wife).

Further afield **Oxted Place** and **Perrysfield** were the main new developments, both early in the century, with many extensions or renovations to the Crown, Oxted Court, and smaller houses in the neighbourhood.

The increasing population meant that **Beadles Lane County First School** was opened in 1872, with the name carved on the gable 'Oxtead National Schools 1872'. This was established as a church school - the schools were called National Schools because they were founded by the National Society which was Church of England. (The new Board Schools which started about this time were non-denominational.) For the 'Oxtead National Schools' the Earl of Cottenham gave the land to the rector and churchwardens. By 1902 it had to be enlarged to take 250 pupils. Accommodation for the head teacher was built at right angles on the end, so that from the front it looked like an ordinary attractive house. For the later history of this school which became St Mary's, see Chapter Six.

Industries

One of the most important buildings was **Oxted Mill** which is actually two mills joined together. They are not on the site of one of those mentioned in the Domesday Book, but a mill must have existed here by at least 1291. Both the present buildings were constructed in the 19C, of red brick with slate roofs. The older one is the smaller, built in about the middle of the century, and has a luccam (or lucomb) for loading the grain over the doorway. It has an overshot 12ft. diameter millwheel of iron which is 5ft. 6in. across.

For the adjoining more recent mill we have an exact date, 1893, and even the hour when it started working - 3 p.m. on 12 June. The miller at the time was called William Heasman, who also owned Coltsford Mill, and he decided to build an up-to-date roller mill on to the existing building. This was driven by a turbine of 4ft. diameter, which turned at 60 revolutions per minute and generated 34hp.

In 1951 both mills ceased to function and the buildings have been used for various enterprises, including as a private house, since then. The millstones outside leaning against the wall are of the French Burr type, used for milling fine flour.

In wintertime the ice would be taken from the mill-pond and stored in the 'ice well' or 'ice house' in Icehouse Wood, hence the name of the present road. The ice stayed frozen all year in its underground store with only the domed roof showing. This shape over centuries has been found to lose less heat than others. The brick dome would have been insulated with thick turf and possibly thatch.

There was always a certain danger of flooding from the pond, notably in 1958 when even some houses in Woodhurst Lane were flooded and in 1968 when a nearby bridge was demolished. For more information on watermills in general and on Coltsford Mill see Chapter Three.

The cottage next door is the **Mill Cottage** which looks several centuries old. It was indeed originally built in the early part of the 18C but was destroyed by a flying bomb in the war and rebuilt in 1951.

The **limeworks** was an important part of commercial life of the town. It is thought that this quarry has been worked for over two centuries yielding greystone chalk of high quality which could be burnt to provide lime, but it was only in the 19C that it became really productive. The Oxted Greystone Lime Company installed a lime hydration plant to produce slaked lime for building and they also supplied quicklime to various trades, as well as fertiliser. Almost all the chalk was quarried by hand until the 1930s when the first mechanical shovels were brought in. Before that there were times when as many as 100 men had to be employed. Old postcards show a line of conical kilns striding across the quarry, which remained in use until comparatively recently. The kilns were built of brick and as they needed constant repair a brickmaker was employed on site. The company had its own railway line to transport the products to the station (see below). Now a part of the quarry has reverted to nature, and plants and butterflies have moved in.

The Oxted Railway

Through most of the 19C life in Oxted continued on its tranquil way. But in 1884 the railway was completed and everything changed. There was an explosion of building round the new station - suddenly Oxted was within commuting and visiting distance of London. 'New' Oxted was born. It might have been born sooner if the railway had not been delayed for 20 years.

In 1865 an Act of Parliament was passed sanctioning the building of a railway from Croydon to Oxted and on to join the Tunbridge Wells and Uckfield line. This line, called the Surrey and Sussex Junction Railway, made encouraging progress at first. Workers dug the Oxted tunnel which is 2261 yards long, and two other tunnels, and built bridges. One was a short distance south of the Oxted tunnel and carried a road to the limeworks - some of the crumbling brickwork can be seen today. The viaduct near Woldingham was also built at this time, and is of brick, unlike later viaducts where iron was used. However, all sorts of problems beset the company, financial and labour difficulties as well as accusations of 'irregularities' regarding the purchase of land, and the whole enterprise lapsed in 1869.

Nearly ten years later, in 1878, another Act enabled work to start again, this time to construct what was now to be known as the Croydon, Oxted and East Grinstead Railway. This was to be owned jointly by the London, Brighton and South Coast Railway and the South Eastern Railway from South Croydon to Crowhurst Junction North, and from thence southwards to be owned solely by the L.B.S.C.R.

Because it was built later than many other lines, certain difficulties arose. For example, the Caterham Railway ran along the bottom of the Caterham

Postcard of Oxted Railway Station of 1910. Notice the milk churns waiting for collection and the typical advertisement for Epps's Cocoa

Oxted Railway Station today

55

valley so this one had to be accommodated on a higher level cut from the valley side. Tunnels, cuttings and viaducts had to be constructed to deal with steep gradients and valleys.

The Croydon, Oxted and East Grinstead Railway was finally opened officially on 12 March 1884. Then in 1888 the branch line to Uckfield was completed. In 1886 a narrow-gauge line, known as the Oxted

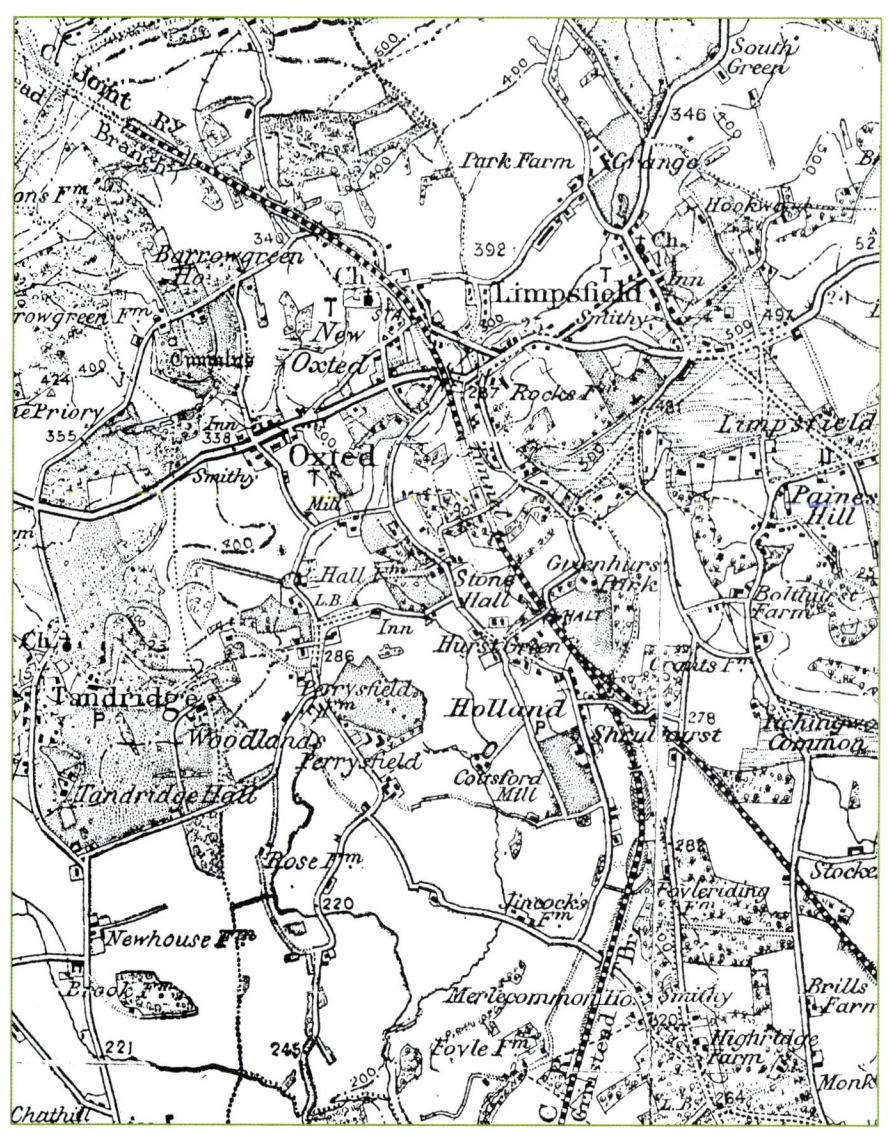

Map of Oxted showing the railway, 'New Oxted' and the Halt at Hurst Green

Limeworks Railway, was constructed for the Oxted Greystone Lime Co., with a siding beside the main line. The line ceased to be used in 1939, and the track was finally lifted in 1969, then the siding in 1971, to make way for the station car-park.

In 1896 the company advertised Oxted as 'a station serving a singularly picturesque and salubrious rural district which promises to become a favourite centre for villa residences'. (Roger Brasier in *Limpsfield Ancient and Modern* quotes this nice example of 19C advertising.) In 1889 a waiting room was constructed at a cost of £90, and in 1891 gas lighting was installed. The station was first called Oxted and Limpsfield since it was half way between Old Oxted and Limpsfield, but soon it found itself in the centre of the new town, so it became simply Oxted Station.

In 1907 a station called Hurst Green Halt was opened for the new commuters south of the A25. The present Hurst Green station was opened in 1961 just to the north of Hurst Green Halt.

The line retained steam trains longer than any other south of London, and it was not until 1962 that the first diesel-powered train arrived here. In 1987 the line to East Grinstead was electrified, but the Uckfield branch line is still diesel operated.

Over the years, 'specials' have been run for various categories of traveller - race-goers, hop-pickers and ramblers, with occasional troop trains. But Oxted station also attracted the unwelcome attentions of the militant supporters of women's suffrage who in 1913 put the makings of a bomb in the gents' toilet. Fortunately nobody was hurt. It was later discovered that one of the perpetrators was no less a figure than the famous Professor H.I. Laski of the London School of Economics. (One might speculate why such a man was not more efficient in carrying out his purpose.)

Buses

Bus services did not begin until the 20C, but it is appropriate to describe them here. In 1914 the East Surrey Traction Company began calling at Oxted on its way from Reigate to Sevenoaks. It promised 'delightful omnibus trips among charming Surrey and Kent scenery'. There were eight buses each way on weekdays and three each way on Sundays. The low railway bridge at Oxted was a bugbear: passengers on the tall open-topped double-deckers had to get out and walk as the buses edged their way through. Even in 1934 special low buses were used to cope with the bridge.

The Hoskins Arms Hotel

Development after the Railway

In December 1886 the Westerham Herald reported that a new hotel was almost finished, a gas holder had been built and the number of lamps had been increased from two to five - clearly a sign of great sophistication. Water pipes were being laid and a branch bank was open three days a week. The reporter predicted that 'the quiet little village will soon become a place of importance.'

Development directly attributable to the railway included the **Hoskins Arms Hotel** which opened in 1892 to cater for the new influx of railway travellers. It was owned by Charles Hoskins Master and was a solid rectangular building with gables and bay windows. Since then of course we have had the circular Hoskins Arms which was burnt out, and now a circular block of flats. A short distance behind the hotel on Church Lane was the thriving **cattle market**, held every Tuesday.

Hoskins Road once led to a sand-pit exploited for building purposes, but houses were also built here. The two pretty plasterwork gables with scrolls and foliage on numbers 2 and 4 bear the date AD 1892 - no. 2 was used as a constituency office by Geoffrey (now Lord) Howe when he was MP for the area. When railway sidings were planned so that coal and chalk could be brought to the new railway, much of the sand was taken away to be used for building.

To keep the inhabitants of the new town in order, in 1894 it was thought expedient to build the **Police Station**, which cost £8000. It had living quarters for single police officers in the part facing Church Lane, cells and a courtroom. By 1912 it was staffed by a superintendent and three constables. In 1995 there was considerable reorganisation within the local area and among other changes policemen no longer live on the premises.

Another sign of the times was the institution of **Oxted Parish Council**, along with others, in the same year, 1894. (This followed the Local Government Act of 1888 whereby elected County Councils were established. Together with the fact that agricultural labourers were given the vote in 1884, this heralded the end of the power of the lords of the manor, held for centuries.) Parish Councils of course have different boundaries from those of parishes centred on churches, and have different functions - they oversee, for example, burial grounds, open spaces, footpaths, playing fields and lighting. One of their first tasks was to organise the enclosure of a part of Hurst Green common land for the building of St Agatha's Hall in 1895, for which they had to obtain a licence from the lord of the manor. Oxted parish, like others in the area, is long and narrow north to south. It

The block of flats on the site of the Hoskins Arms Hotel. Compare the traffic on Station Road West with the previous illustration

stretches from north of the M25 down to Caterfield Bridge in the south, but is closely bounded by Tandridge on the west and Limpsfield on the east, roughly four miles north to south by one mile at its narrowest. This reflects the shape of Tandridge district itself, whose boundaries almost correspond to the thousand-year-old boundaries of the Saxon hundred.

Another amenity for the developing town was the formation of sports clubs - the **Oxted Cricket Club** was formed in 1890 and the **Oxted and District Football Club** in 1894.

Hurst Green as we know it today began to grow around the station Hurst Green Halt, a little to the south of the present station of Hurst Green.

St Agatha's Hall, the Church Hall of St John's, was built in 1895 as a mission room. There already was a mission hall on the green which it is thought had been used for some time as lodging for the workers on the new railway. As just mentioned above, Charles Hoskins Master the lord of the manor granted a licence for the new hall, necessary since it meant building on common land. It was called St Agatha's probably after the daughter of Mr and Mrs Hussey who financed the building - she died young. The hall was used as a church until St John's was built in 1913 and again after the fire in St John's in 1988. Now known affectionately as Aggies on the Green, it is open at certain times for coffees and light lunches, staffed by volunteers, as well as being the venue for social events and club meetings.

St Silvan's Chapel, picturesquely sited by Staffhurst Wood, began life as a mission room in 1898. For its building, land was donated by the lord of the manor and the cost was met by contributions from people in the neighbourhood. It was consecrated as a church in 1930, and in 1976 it was adapted so that one part could accommodate the priest in charge.

Ridgeway House (Blunt House) is on the corner of Barrow Green Road and Sandy Lane. Now a nursing home, it was built in 1887 in neo-Georgian style by John Oldrid Scott. Modelled on Blunt House, Croydon (1760), the house contains richly decorated plaster ceilings and door surrounds from the Croydon house. John Oldrid was chairman of Oxted Parish Council 1901-8 and lived here until 1913. He also designed St John's, Hurst Green, in 1913 in a neo-Gothic style. He was the son of Sir George Gilbert Scott, the renowned Gothic revival architect who designed the Albert Memorial and St Pancras Station. Another of this architecturally talented family was Giles Gilbert Scott, grandson of George.

Rooks Nest, now Streete Court School in Tandridge, a listed 18C building in classical style with an imposing portico can be seen from the A25, opposite the garden centre. **Sir George Gilbert Scott** lived there for three years from 1869. There were four in the family and they needed ten servants to look after them. Sir George was responsible for 'restoring' an enormous number of old churches, including those at Tandridge and Godstone. Rooks Nest passed to other owners - in 1918 an M.P. who lived there was fined £400 for hoarding food. He had a stock of 37 weeks' supply of tea and 106lb of rice among much else. A telling indication of house prices is that the property fetched £70,000 when it was sold in 1927.

The Master Family

The lord of the manor or squire was still a power to be reckoned with in the 19C. After Katherine Hoskins married Lech Master in the late 18C, the Master family dominated life in the town for over a hundred years. The Master coat of arms consists of three griffons' heads.

The following is a table showing the Master family memorials in St Mary's Church.

Masters memorials in St Mary's

1807	Katherine	relict of Lech Master of Lancaster, daughter of William Hoskins
1814	Rev Lech Hoskins Master	son of Katherine and Lech
1854	Louise	wife of Charles Lech Hoskins Master age 63
1878	Edward Hoskins	born 1840, second son of Charles Hoskins Master (window)
1892	Emily	wife of Charles Hoskins Master age 72 (window)
1903	Louisa Henrietta	age 53, second daughter of Charles (window)
1908	Katherine Emily Hoskins Bengough	age 62, elder daughter of Charles Hoskins and Emily Master (also window)

Idyllic Hurst Green. The signpost points to Oxted on the left and Edenbridge and Lingfield to the right

The churchyard of St Mary's

There are also memorials to the Hoskins Master family in the churchyard, including those of Charles Hoskins Master and his wife Emily, and Edward Hoskins Master (died 1878). The latter has another memorial, mentioned above, inside the church.

Not just the family but their servants are remembered - there is the grave of Thomas Sayer who died in 1873 at the age of 77, who for 40 years was a 'faithful servant' to Charles Hoskins Master of Barrow Green House.

Other working people are recorded in memorials here. One commemorates a porter called Thomas Betteridge who had worked at Oxted Station for nine years and who died in 1898, evidently after an accident at South Bermondsey Station, with the verse:

> Life's railway o'er each station past
>
> In death I stopped and rest at last.

The wife of William Tarrant the brickmaker of Hurst Green who died in 1882 has an imposing tombstone. There is also William Heasman and his wife and daughter, the family who owned the mills.

Judith Lashmar the brewer of the High Street is buried in a large railed family tomb with her husband John and their daughter Sarah, their son William and William's wife, together with another member of the family, Audrey Ann Lashmar. There are other Lashmar graves as well. Lt. Col. Francis Bellis (1824) and Robert Martin Leake (1833) also have impressive railed tombs.

Literary Figures in Oxted

The railway had made the journey from London so easy that it became fashionable to retreat to rural areas. Prominent people could now afford to have a house in the country and be assured that they were not cutting themselves off from London arts and culture. Many famous people passed through Oxted station on their way to their country retreats or to visit friends.

Stephen Crane 1871-1900

Crane was an American writer who lived for a few months in Oxted. His first novel was the notorious *Maggie: A Girl of the Streets*. *The Red Badge of Courage* his powerful next novel about a young soldier at war and his first book of poetry *The Black Riders* brought him more respectable fame. He was a war correspondent in Greece and it was when he returned from there in 1897 that he and Cora Taylor, a brothel-keeper, settled together for a short time in Limpsfield and then at Ravensbrook in Oxted, a house entered by way of its own lodge from the bottom of Snatts Hill. He was permanently in debt to the

Blue House Road, now Bluehouse Lane. These two postcards show the leisurely pace of life at the turn of the century

local tradesmen. Stephen went off in April 1898 to report on the war in Cuba. In January 1899 he returned and was besieged by creditors, who included the landlord to whom he owed £91 for a year's rent. After a year or so he died of TB and malarial fever contracted in Cuba. He is mainly remembered for his realism and his accomplished short stories, of which the best is judged to be *The Bride comes to Yellow Sky*.

Joseph Conrad (1857-1924)

Conrad's visit with his wife and baby was short - they came to stay for a few days with the Cranes in 1898, and a photograph survives to prove it. Edward Garnett (see below) came over from Limpsfield to Oxted to see them, and the Conrads then went to stay with him.

W.H. Davies (1871-1940)

The poet and author of *The Autobiography of a Supertramp* often visited Edward Garnett at Limpsfield and later came to live briefly in Oxted in a villa called Malpas House, possibly on the area occupied by Johnsdale today.

Limpsfield and the Fabians

The Fabians were an association of intellectuals who hoped to change society by peaceful means. They included George Bernard Shaw, H.G. Wells and Sidney and Beatrice Webb. One of the founder members was Edward Pease who lived in Limpsfield and wrote a history of the society. Edward and Constance Garnett were a publisher's reader and a translator who were interested in Fabian ideas, and when they moved to The Cearne in Limpsfield Chart in 1896, the railway provided an easy means for friends to come from London to visit. Among those thus attracted were John Galsworthy, D.H. Lawrence, Hilaire Belloc, W.H. Davies, W.H. Hudson, Shaw, the Webbs, H.E. Bates and Ford Madox Ford.

These people would take the train to Oxted or Edenbridge and then would either walk or be driven to Limpsfield, to enjoy what Shaw called the 'jolly Fabian domesticity at Limpsfield'. A letter from D.H. Lawrence to Garnett in 1911 says that he will arrive in Oxted by the 6.32 train and will then walk to Limpsfield. Later, in 1930, Arthur Rackham (1867-1939), the great illustrator of Shakespeare, Dickens, Barrie and Kenneth Grahame, also came to live in Limpsfield and was friendly with the Fabian group.

Aggies on the Green

So it is that by the end of the 19C Oxted is ready to embrace all the conveniences of the rail connection to London, and to switch the focus and centre of the town to a new location.

Caxton House, Station Road West

The Barn Theatre constructed from medieval timbers

Chapter Five

The Twentieth Century

As we have seen, the foundations of New Oxted were laid in the late 19C. The 20C completes the story with the expansion of the modern shopping and business centre, but on a site a mile away and separated from the old town by the A25. Old Oxted has developed too, in a way which preserves its character.

New Building

The first wave of development of the new part of Oxted was sparked off by the coming of the railway in 1884. At that time it was necessary to develop utilitarian building fairly rapidly, but when the first spurt of construction was over, the early 1900s saw a more considered approach. Now there was leisure to think of the decorative and the picturesque, something that would express the character of the new town and at the same time link it in style with Old Oxted. As so often happens, the right man, or rather the right family, was on the spot at the right time. Just at this juncture a family of builders called Williams happened to be in the area and one after another they were responsible for a distinctive style which has been called Oxted Mock Tudor. They were later joined by a gifted wood-carver called Charlie Payne and a pupil of his, Harry Whitner, who excelled at the decorative detail.

One of the first buildings was **Caxton House**, the block on the end of Station Road West across the road from the police station. For some time there was a printing business here, hence no doubt the appropriate name of Caxton House, after the 15C printer. John Williams built this in the early 1900s. He had come from Australia and had worked on several large houses in England before coming to Oxted. The block has almost every possible Tudor device, tall chimneys, three different gables, two dormers, half-timbering and galleries, together with handsome doors.

(The large rusting anchor on the pavement at the next corner was put there to advertise the fish shop which once occupied the corner premises.)

Further up on the same side the two blocks from the corner of Hoskins Road are equally decorative. The first, from about 1900, has Venetian style triple windows, and ironwork on the balcony, the next is adorned with a wealth of carving, with grotesque heads, owls, balusters, balconies and decorated

Station Road West a hundred years ago

Station Road West today

barge-boards. This was built in 1933 by Bentley Williams to a design by Ivan Roberts. The next few shops also have some intriguing details. The block on the end nearest the station has a plasterwork gable and the words 'Oxted Corn Store Berry & Sons'. Round the corner under a brick Dutch gable the faded letters of the word 'Refreshments' are legible, strategically placed to catch the eye of thirsty commuters.

Across the road, the **Plaza Cinema** was built in 1930. This was to replace the old cinema in the grounds of the Hoskins Arms Hotel, which had a humble tin roof but showed the latest films of the time - Tom Mix, Felix and the Keystone Cops. The new building was luxurious in comparison, and is thought to have been built by C.A. Williams. This is the Oxted Tudor style in its more developed, decorative phase, with carvings of vines, grapes and palm-leaves on the timbers. Inside, the decoration recalls a subdued Art Deco style, with pilasters and lights that have an Egyptian feel. The cinema kept open during World War II, and if there was an air raid a red warning light would come on so that people could leave if they wished to take cover. It is nostalgic to record that in 1970 the cost of a ticket was 3s. The old ticket-machine is still there, built into the counter in the foyer.

Other buildings on this side are not so lavish in their decoration, but still repay observation, with their handsome wooden carved doors, their gables and half-timbering. The **Post Office** was opened in 1915 - it was previously in the next door building to the right.

In Station Road East it is the **NatWest Bank** that catches the eye with its carved timbers and unusual shell-like overdoor. This was built by Bentley Williams and carved by Charlie Payne. Further up the hill are other examples of the style with galleries, arcades, and more half-timbering, set off by a little garden.

The attractive **Barn Theatre** on Bluehouse Lane was constructed using material from a medieval sawmill which once stood in Limpsfield. It was probably originally built as a barn and then converted to a sawmill. The building was dismantled, and the wood and the large quantity of roof-tiles were used for the theatre. It was opened in 1924 as a local community theatre with the aim of linking Oxted and Limpsfield as a venue for social events. During World War II it was occupied by the army, so that afterwards a new start was required. Friends of the Barn (FOBS) now work actively to support the theatre. The two companies which are resident are the **Oxted Players**, formerly the Student Players, who present drama, and the **Oxted Operatic Society** which gives musical productions, and there are visiting companies as well. It seats 248 and has a stage of 24ft. by 18ft., and backstage are three

The NatWest Bank with a wealth of carving in the Oxted Mock Tudor style

dressing-rooms and a kitchen. The Barn has its own scenery and props, as well as dry ice and smoke machines. Famous people who have appeared there over the years are Dame Flora Robson, Lady Violet Bonham-Carter, Randolph Churchill, Michael Tippett, Ray Allen and Lord Charles, Roy Castle, Ronnie Corbett, Richard Stilgoe and Jimmie Tarbuck. For the new expansion plans, see Chapter Six.

Town Farm occupied the triangle between Church Lane and the A25, and is still shown on a postcard from 1908. The Hay Wain hotel soon occupied the site and this was sold in 1939. After that came the present Langley House, now Surrey Oaklands NHS Trust. (See back cover.)

Hurst Green continued to grow in the pre-war years and a school was needed. **Merle Common School** was opened in 1912 under the sponsorship of Marjory Pease, wife of Edward Pease of the Fabian Society. (See Chapter Four.) Her portrait hangs in Tandridge District Council offices. This was the first school in Surrey to offer school dinners. The building, no longer a school, stands beside the railway bridge in Merle Common Road.

Master Park which was given to the people of Oxted in 1923

The 20ft. high **War Memorial** of Portland Stone beside Master Park shows 77 names of victims of World War I and 41 from World War II, and nine civilians. The land for this was given by Charles Hoskins Master, and it cost £402 11s. 2p. in voluntary contributions, which was finally paid off in 1922. Of the local soldiers killed in World War I almost 60% served in the Queen's West Surrey Regiment.

The War Memorial beside Master Park with 127 names of local people who died in the two World Wars

Master Park came into being in 1923. Charles Hoskins Master gave 'Marls Field....laid out and preserved for ever thereafter for the healthy recreation and amusement of the inhabitants of Oxted and their friends.' Cricket, tennis and football can be played, and a new children's playground has been proposed. The park is not owned by the council, but is run by trustees and a Management Committee and is supported mainly by voluntary contributions since no maintenance fund was set up at the time of the gift.

The group of houses in **Johnsdale** was also built between the wars.

In Old Oxted the **High Street** was surfaced with tarmacadam in 1925. The **Brew House Flats** were erected in 1936 on the site of Lashmar's brewery and some other old buildings which were demolished. The brewery was originally built in the 15C and had many extensions and renovations. The flats were set back from the road because at that time it was thought that the street could be widened all along its length, but of course with the growing consciousness of the value of historic houses this idea had to be abandoned.

Memorials in the Churchyard of St Mary's

In 1986 St Mary's celebrated its 900th anniversary. No one really knows when the church was founded - it is certainly older than that, but in common with other churches first mentioned in the Domesday Book of 1086 it seemed fitting to mark the year as a centenary. As well as the two plaques inside the church previously described, Bishop Bowlby of Southwark planted a tree in the churchyard for the occasion. There are also two trees planted by Mohamed al Fahed in memory of his son Dodi and Princess Diana.

In the churchyard there are gravestones which commemorate several of the Hoskins Master family who died in the 20C, including Herbert Francis Hoskins Master, died 1967, Charles Hoskins Master, died 1935, Beatrice Hoskins Master, died 1966, and Charles Edward Hoskins Master, died 1960. A tall neo-Gothic monument to the east of the church commemorates Katherine Emily Hoskins who died in 1908 and has the dedication:

> In memory of all who rest in this churchyard and of Katherine Emily Hoskins, eldest daughter of Charles Hoskins Master of Barrow Green Oxted and for 22 years wife of Major E.B. Bengough. She died on 27th June 1908 aged 62 years. The souls of the righteous are in the hand of God.

One or two military tombstones are also there, such as that of Carey Saunders who died at the Ypres Salient in 1915, buried in the family grave almost obscured by a large yew tree, and E.J. Baker of the Worcestershire Regiment who died in April 1918.

The Nightingales of Foyle Riding

In 1998 a CD was released with recordings of the cellist Beatrice Harrison playing in the garden of Foyle Riding to the accompaniment of the local nightingales - a cassette had already been issued. The talented sisters May, Beatrice, Monica and Margaret Harrison lived at Foyle Riding, south of Hurst Green, from 1922 to 1936. All were musically gifted - May and Margaret played the violin, Beatrice the cello and Monica was a singer, and of course all four played the piano as well.

One evening Beatrice found that when she played the cello in the garden, the nightingales joined in, and when she managed to persuade the BBC to do an outside broadcast it was the first time it had been done. Soon Beatrice and the nightingales were a regular feature on night-time radio. (The nightingales' song had actually been captured on a wax cylinder way back around the turn of the century. At that time they were said to respond to a train whistle from Oxted Station or even the rattle of a can of stones.)

The Harrison sisters were well known and highly regarded in the world of music. Beatrice often played Elgar's *Cello Concerto* under the direction of the composer himself. In fact she became so famous that her sister Margaret gave up her own career to help organise and accompany Beatrice's tours. May was described as the world's greatest woman violinist by no less an authority than Fritz Kreisler, and Delius' *Third Violin Sonata* was dedicated to her. Delius also dedicated his *Double Concerto* to May and Beatrice, and his *Cello Sonata* to Beatrice, who was described by the respected music critic Ernest Newman as the best British cellist. Monica however did not achieve such fame, largely owing to ill-health, but Roger Quilter dedicated his *Pastoral Songs* to her. The sisters toured all over the world and composers such as Arnold Bax, Percy Grainger and John Ireland as well as Delius and Quilter created music for them. Through their work the sisters also made friends with those in the highest and most influential circles, such as Princess Victoria the sister of George V, who joined in a private recording with herself accompanying Margaret and Beatrice in Elgar's *Salut d'Amour*. The last of the sisters, Margaret, died in 1995 at 96.

Station Road East

Station Road West

75

When Beatrice and May were playing Brahms' *Double Concerto* with Sir Thomas Beecham in a Hallé concert, they met Delius and the two families became friendly, visiting each other when Delius lived in Grez, in France. After Delius' death May went to see his widow Jelka Delius who said that Delius had wished to be buried in one of those little churchyards in southern England which reminded him of Gray's *Elegy in a Country Churchyard*. The poem was the basis of his last cello work *Elegy*. As May's mother was buried at Limpsfield she suggested this spot and it was arranged. Sir Thomas Beecham delivered the oration at the graveside, and in fact he too was later buried in the same churchyard. Other musical celebrities laid to rest in Limpsfield are Eileen Joyce and Norman del Mar, as well as all four Harrison sisters and their parents. May, Beatrice and Monica Harrison are laid in the same grave, but Margaret is buried with her parents'.

Their memory is kept alive by the Harrison Sisters' Players, who concentrate on playing works of composers associated with the Harrisons.

Memories from between the Wars

The leisurely years between the two world wars yield mixed memories which recall the flavour of life before technology which is still remembered by some of our residents. Here are a few varied reminiscences with some features which we are very glad to be rid of and others we would like to see again.

In the years between the two World Wars, Old Oxted was almost self-sufficient in its shops, and deliveries were made every day from food shops. Other items delivered on a Saturday were fish and chips, and also muffins and crumpets. These were carried in a huge wicker basket and the delivery man walked a round of 20 miles, ringing a bell to alert customers.

At Oxted and Limpsfield station, passengers were greeted by the Stationmaster in peaked cap and gold-braided uniform, plus Head Porter and other porters, Ticket Collector and Ticket Office Clerk. At that time coal, building and corn merchants and their products were much in evidence, and the cattle from the cattle market held every Tuesday also travelled by rail.

In the 20s and early 30s most houses were lit by gas. Oxted had three gasholders, replaced in the 1960s by the present large one (possibly soon to be removed). The Oxted and Limpsfield Gas Company later became the Croydon Company - besides gas they produced coal, tar and fertiliser.

The veterinary surgeons' practice in Barrow Green Road has been there under different names since this period and their quarantine facilities were used to hold the animals presented to the royal family.

The library was first in the old St Mary's Hall situated in Church Lane, and in the late 1930s moved to a tin hut, in what was the Godstone Rural District Council Offices complex, where Tandridge District Council now is.

Ballroom dancing was very popular and possible in many venues. Hoskins Arms Hotel, the Barn Theatre, the old St Mary's Hall and St Agatha's Hall were a few of them.

At that time there were many jobs available for gardeners and chauffeurs, and the railways and buses needed staff. Local builders, the limeworks, the gas works, and farming also provided jobs, and deliverymen were needed by the shops. For women there were places as domestics to the gentry and as typists, while at Hurst Green there was the laundry and a factory which produced unbreakable gramophone records, the Vitreo Colloid Works.

*(With thanks to **Mr Bert Critcher** and **Mr Bert Atkinson** for these memories.)*

Oxted in World War II

As Oxted was so close to London it saw quite a lot of enemy activity. There are remains of bomb craters in Staffhurst Wood - the bombs were presumably aimed at an arms depot in the wood established by the Canadian forces. There were four Canadian regiments stationed in Oxted and they were billeted all over the town in the larger houses. In order to deceive the German planes, a dummy aerodrome was established near the quarry with flashing lights to simulate activity there. Another precaution was the balloon barrage on fields beside the railway. The kilns in the chalk pit had to be blacked out as well since their fires would have provided a useful landmark for the enemy. Local residents with long memories can recall hearing a bomb falling on numbers 4 and 6 Peter Avenue which killed several people, and one resident was living in Tandridge Priory Cottage when the Germans tried to bomb the Priory - not a pleasant experience. Others did fire duty which meant walking up and down the streets armed with a stirrup-pump ready to extinguish fires. The ARP was also active in the town, and one member recalls watching for doodlebugs on the field where Somerfields now is. In the Godstone Rural District as a whole casualties from flying bombs were: 25 killed, 213 injured, as well as 54 buildings destroyed and 160 damaged.

The **9th Surrey (Oxted) Battalion Home Guard**, as it eventually became, had its beginnings on 14 May 1940 when the Chief Constable of Surrey telephoned Oxted Police Station notifying him of the coming broadcast calling for volunteers.

The Oxted and Godstone Company was formed with a platoon from each of the main parishes, and the company had headquarters in Limpsfield and Godstone. By the end of 1940 there were 198 members. The area covered by the Oxted group stretched roughly from Tandridge village to Staffhurst Wood, and from the chalk pit to the Godstone Railway line. The stand-down ceremony was held in Master Park on 3 December 1944, with 180 members.

> **Mr Bert Critcher remembers:** The Oxted unit of the Home Guard met every Tuesday evening in the Church Hall in Church Lane for arms drill and other instruction, then we did marches and so on. Night exercises were often on Tandridge golf course, where a lantern on a green had to be stolen without discovery by the defending 'troops'. This was a popular venue as the clever few were always at the rear and when we marched up the village they dropped off at the Wheatsheaf for a quick pint and hurried back via a short cut so they arrived at the same time as the main column. Each section had a scout, a man who knew the area very well, and one of these was a farmworker who turned up with a shotgun as well as a rifle. After dumping his rifle he would shoot rabbits and pheasants with his shotgun, which were a very welcome addition to the meagre meat ration. If any failed to stay the course they were left to be collected on the way back, and some wonderful games of Solo were enjoyed by those who dropped out. One night as the group were meeting in a room below a flat, a very senior member managed to let off his rifle through the ceiling and into the flat. The meeting-place was soon moved!

Major Robert Henry Cain lived in Oxted for some years in the late 1960s and the early 1970s. He was awarded the VC for his extraordinary courage, endurance and leadership at the Battle of Arnhem in 1944, when his company of the South Staffordshire Regiment (Airborne) was cut off from the rest. Major Cain held the position for six days, and although wounded inflicted severe damage on the enemy troops and equipment, so that they were demoralised and retreated.

The name of a young woman who went to school in Limpsfield should be recorded here. **Diana Hope Rowden** attended Manor House School, became a WAAF section officer then worked as a secret agent during the war, and died in a Nazi concentration camp. She was posthumously awarded the MBE, MID and Croix de Guerre and was mentioned in dispatches.

Notable Residents

Sir Ernest Benn lived in Oxted and died in 1954. He was the publisher whose Sixpenny Library and Sixpenny Poets were among the first popular series of paperback educational books. He took over management of the family publishing business before he was 21 and enlarged it to include hardcover and paperback books. Ernest Benn Ltd became the publisher of the *Blue Guides*, the respected cultural guide-books, now published by A.& C. Black. Benn was an author himself - he wrote *The Confessions of a Capitalist* (1925), *Governed to Death* (pamphlet, 1948), and *The State the Enemy* (1953).

Martin Coles Harman, a colourful character known as the 'King of Lundy', was living in Oxted when he died in 1954. Harman was a bankrupt and discredited businessman. In 1925 he somehow managed to buy the island of Lundy, in the Bristol Channel off the northern coast of Devon for £16,000. Here he made all the laws and issued his own stamps and coins with his portrait. The unit of currency was the 'puffin' which equalled a penny.

Leslie Kenneth O'Brien, Lord O'Brien of Lothbury, (1908-1995) became Chief Cashier of the Bank of England in 1955, and so his signature on our banknotes was one of the most familiar in the land. He became Deputy Governor of the Bank of England, and then Governor. He lived in Oxted from 1989 until his death.

T.E.B. Clarke (1907-1989), the screen-writer of many Ealing comedies, also lived in Oxted. He wrote the scripts for, among others, *The Lavender Hill Mob*, *The Titfield Thunderbolt* and *Passport to Pimlico*, besides writing for such prestigious films as *The Blue Lamp*, *A Tale of Two Cities* and *Sons and Lovers*.

Commander John Simon Kerans DSO, RN (1915-1985) lived in Oxted from 1980 until his death. He was the commander of HMS Amethyst in April 1949 when she sailed up the Yangtze with supplies for the British Embassy in Nanjing. The ship was caught in the crossfire of the civil war battle raging across the river and it was July before she could escape again.

Commander Kerans was awarded the DSO immediately by King George VI, who also sent the welcome message 'Splice the mainbrace!'

Mohamed al Fahed is the owner of Barrow Green Court on Barrow Green Road. He was born in Alexandria in Egypt in the 1930s, and is now one of the most successful businessmen in the world, owning the House of Fraser, which includes Harrods, and the magazine Punch, to name just two of his acquisitions. After the death of Diana Princess of Wales and al Fahed's son Dodi on 31 August 1997, heaps of flowers were laid at the gates of Barrow Green Court by local people. Dodi was later buried on the estate and, as mentioned above, his father planted two trees in the graveyard of St Mary's Church in remembrance of Diana and Dodi.

The musician **Harold Darke** (1888-1976) while staying for Christmas 1911 with the Calkin family in Bluehouse Lane composed the music for one of our favourite carols *In the Bleak Midwinter* (for which Gustav Holst also composed a melody). The words are from a poem by Christina Rossetti.

The **Cockburns** of Cockburns Port owned Bonally House, which later became for a time the Midland Bank Training College.

Several famous people lived in nearby Limpsfield - Field-Marshal Sir William Slim, Eileen Joyce, Jeremy Thorpe, Sir Michael Tippett and the McDougalls of the flour company.

Lives of Local People

Mrs Millie Trinder has lived in Oxted almost all her life. She was known to hundreds of residents as 'Millie the Milk' because for 25 years she delivered the milk for Lenton's Dairy on the corner opposite the Old Bell. She began to work for Lenton's in the early years of the war and had to cycle in the blackout from Pollard's Oak to get to the dairy by 6.30a.m. Later she moved to Old Oxted where she still lives.

The first year she had three days off (but not Christmas) and was first paid £2 a week, later raised to £2 10s. At that time Lenton's had five horses and three motor vans. One of her favourite horses was black, called Bess, who knew exactly where to stop to deliver milk. A woman at the greengrocer's on Station Road East would regularly give Bess carrots, but if she wasn't quick enough in producing them the horse would cross the road against the rules to collect her treat. In summer Bess wore a fetching straw hat with holes for her ears, to keep the flies at bay.

Memorial trees for Princess Diana and Dodi Fahed in St Mary's churchyard

Every second day the milk deliverers had to fill the bottles with milk which had been collected by lorry from surrounding farms and every second day they scrubbed out their vehicles. Neither of these tasks was at all easy or pleasant in a severe winter. The milk round was in two parts - High Street to Wheeler Avenue and Peter Avenue, then Station Road West and Hoskins Road, East Hill and the turn by the Police Station, then it was back to the dairy for fresh supplies. The second half consisted of part of Barrow Green Road and then Station Road East together with its side roads. During the war years the High Street would be clogged with army tanks and lorries since of course there was no A25 or M25, and she often had to wait patiently at the bottom of the hill before she could get back to the dairy. Mrs Trinder was one of the first to drive an electric milk float and one of the few women to do so. It was one of the first heavy models with iron-bound wheels, which made such a noise when on the move that she could not hear when there was an air raid and people would wave and point upwards to alert her to what was going on.

More memories of milk are provided by **Mrs C. Howard** whose husband had a small dairy farm. He milked by hand at 5a.m. and 3p.m., then went out to deliver milk twice a day at 3d. a pint in the summer and 4d. a pint in the winter.

Miss Nellie Dowell worked at Oxted Telephone Exchange from the 1920s until 1957. The exchange overlooked the garden of the Hoskins Arms Hotel as it was on the ground floor of the Post Office. After a few weeks' training she was employed part-time at a wage of 13s. 4d. a week. A year later she became Officer in Charge. Girls worked from 8 a.m. to 8 p.m., when men took over for the night shift. An inspector would arrive in town unannounced and ask subscribers to make a call so she could listen and judge the quality of service. However, the station staff would have already have rung the exchange to warn them of her arrival. People would ring up shops every day with their orders and expected the operator to know which number they wanted without bothering to look up the number. One subscriber asked for The Copse and was not best pleased to be put through to the police station. As at that time the four doctors in Oxted worked from their homes, much ingenuity was required to be able to find them in an emergency if they were out on their rounds.

They were often asked questions which ranged from 'What's on at the cinema?' and 'Which chemist is on duty?' to 'How do I cook haddock?' from a lone male.

Oxted School, formerly Oxted County School. This part is the original building of 1929

When the war started more staff and equipment were needed, and they had to receive and pass on air raid messages to other exchanges, the police, the fire station who sounded the siren and the ARP. By the end of the war the staff had increased from four to 16.

The automatic exchange in Barrow Green Road opened in 1957 and thus ended an era of personal service and human interest.

Mr Stanley Brown was a JP for 20 years, and Chairman of the Bench for much of that time. The court was first called the Godstone Petty Sessions which later became Oxted Court and sat in the courtroom in the police station. They dealt with the juvenile crime of the area, as well as adoptions and betting licences, which kept them busy one day a fortnight. They were in contact with probation officers, and were able to send boys to Borstal or put them on probation. On the bench was a glass box with a pair of white gloves and on the one and only occasion when there were no cases to be heard Mr Brown was presented with the gloves. Mr Brown was a Chartered Surveyor and auctioneer, and he presided over the monthly auctions in the Barn Theatre. At that time many of the big old houses had to be sold because the owners could no longer afford to maintain them, and the furniture had to

A25 at the entrance to Old Oxted

Sycamore Court Flats

be auctioned. The items ranged from antiques to the mundane trivia of everyday life. Through his work he met several of Oxted's and Limpsfield's famous inhabitants, such as Eileen Joyce and the Cockburn family.

Mrs Irene Barton was one of the very first pupils who started at Oxted School in May 1929. (The school adopted the new name in September 1999.) In 1999 she organised a reunion for all pupils from 1929 to 1949, and 121 of them came to tour the school and reminisce about the old days. The school, that is, the main block visible from the road, had been purpose-built to educate both boys and girls, the first mixed school in Surrey. There were two staircases and two playgrounds for the two sexes, and in the classroom the boys sat on one side and the girls on the other. The Head would cane the boys or give detentions or lines for misdemeanours - Mrs Barton remembers writing out 'Speech is silver but silence is golden' 300 times. At first the pupils had to walk to Master Park for outdoor games but soon the girls had their own playing-fields for hockey, netball and tennis, and the boys had fields for their sports. They had lessons in all the basic subjects, as well as cookery and art, and they had a small orchestra which played for the hymn at the daily assembly. (See also Chapter Six for details of the fire of 1998 and plans for rebuilding.)

Before Oxted School, Mrs Barton went to Beadles Lane School, and remembers at the age of seven or eight being taken to the mill pond to learn to swim, when the field was muddy and full of cows, and the mill pond had an icy stream flowing through it. There was a rough screen of hessian rigged up for the children to change behind. The instructor walked along the bank with a long pole with a strap round the child to help him or her to keep afloat. On Ascension Day there would be a procession to St Mary's Church for a service, with St George, a May Queen and white-clad attendants, followed by the children. She remembers also coming home in winter and meeting the lamp-lighter with his pole to light the gas-lamps. At home they had oil-lamps downstairs and went to bed carrying candles. The toilet was in the back garden, a wooden seat over a deep black hole at the bottom of which was a pan occasionally flushed with tap water. When the pan was full it would tip and empty straight into the sewer.

Post-war Development

The **Oxted and Limpsfield Directory** for 1949 is a mine of information about people, shops and businesses just after the war. It gives lists of every house and every shop and their owners. On the corner of Bluehouse Lane

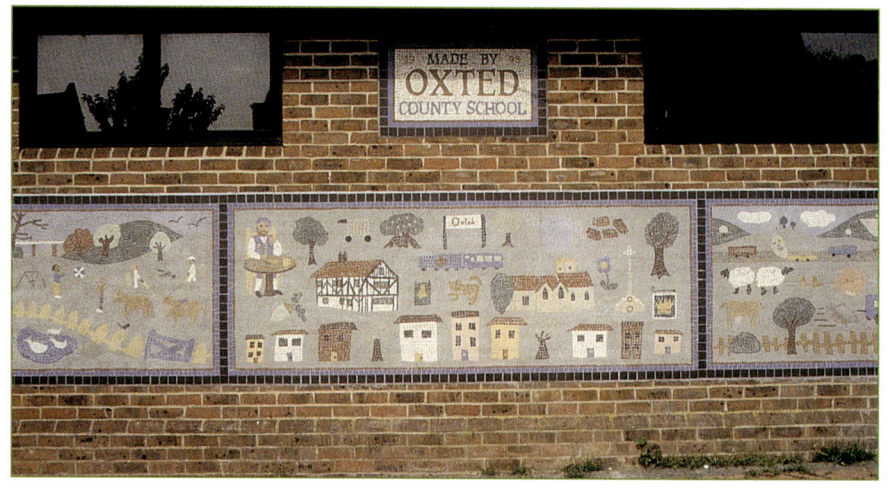

Mosaic by the pupils of Oxted School

and Station Road East was Oxted House, then the rectory, with the Rev C. Pugh living there. At Barrow Green Court there was Capt. C. E. Hoskins Master, and at the Police Station was Supt. A.T. Steeds. Brew House, the block of flats in the High Street, had 12 residents listed. The advertisements are revealing - the Hoskins Arms Hotel boasts of electric fires and hot and cold water in all bedrooms, lock-up garages, tennis courts, bowling green and squash courts as well as a ballroom. Jobs was then an ironmongers selling fertilisers and tools as well as furniture, and Blades was in business then, with the phone number Oxted 17.

Mosaic in the station underpass

Lenton's Model Dairy has an advertisement proclaiming that their milk was tuberculin tested and the shoe shop advertisement has a picture of an X-ray machine and extols its virtues. Signwriters and coal merchants are among the businesses which are now long gone, and there seems to be a garage at every turn. The wording of some advertisements is delightfully old-fashioned - the hairdresser says 'Gentlemen waited upon at their own homes', and 'high-class commodities' are available in several establishments. At this time T.E.B. Clarke was living in Hoskins Road and Sir Ernest Benn in East Hill Road (see above under Notable Residents for more on these well-known Oxted inhabitants).

St Mary's Church Hall and **St Mary's Close** were built in the 1960s and 1970s. Also in the 60s Oxted expanded to the north with the **Silkham Road** estate.

In the early 1970s the **A25** which had run through the High Street was finally banished to a short bypass and a medieval hall house in Brook Lane was demolished to make room for it. This of course was a huge relief for the High Street where the traffic was constantly jammed in the narrow confines of the road.

The station underpass was completely refurbished in 1985 so that a convenient ramp led straight out to Station Road West replacing the steps to be climbed on to the platform. The vivid and imaginative **mosaics** were completed in four stages over a period of years by a Kent firm. Oliver Budd, who started the business with his father, designed the pictorial pieces. The 'Woodland Walk' which leads to the car park has hidden in the design 38

Tandridge Leisure Centre

Safeway Supermarket

creatures including two fairies. The latest additions are two walls and lettering in 1998, and the one on the front of the station by Oxted School.

The **M25** was finally completed in 1986, taking a route of about a twenty-mile radius round London and it is now the busiest motorway in Britain. As it is about a mile from Oxted centre, with some homes being very near indeed, it has had quite an impact, with its hum of traffic. However, it does mean swifter access to the motorway network.

Gatwick Airport was officially opened in 1936 but did not develop rapidly until after the war when foreign holidays and business trips became a normal part of life for so many people. The North Terminal was finished in 1988. Gatwick is the second largest airport in the UK and has nearly 30 million passengers a year. It is very convenient though not (yet) a nuisance as regards noise.

The complex with the **Council Offices, Library** and **Health Centre**, which is in fact not in Oxted but over the border in Limpsfield parish, was built in the 1970s on what had been the site of the old Oxted hospital. By that time, all that was left of the hospital was the mortuary with its tiny high windows, which was used by the Citizens' Advice Bureau. The library was in a make-shift building, as related above. (The present hospital was built in the 1930s - see Chapter Six.)

The 1990s

The large expanse of land beside the station owned by the railway became available and some major additions to the town amenities were built.
Tandridge Leisure Pool was finished in 1990 and draws users from far and wide to its pool, gym and classes and events of all sorts.

When **Safeway** was built in 1996 excavations for the foundations revealed old sleepers from the railway sidings which used to be here, and also the Greensand beds could be seen. Safeway here employs almost 200 people.

The **Oxted Inn** was built shortly after Safeway. No public house had been built in 'New Oxted' because the land was owned first by the Hoskins family estate and then by the Barrow Green Estate Company and the deeds of the land forbade the sale of alcohol, originally to protect the trade of the Hoskins Arms Hotel. In 1964 the Barrow Green Estate Company went into voluntary liquidation, but there are still restrictions in place, so that it was several more years before a new outlet was permitted.

Sycamore Court flats were also built beside the leisure centre to complete the new development with private homes.

Further afield, at **Broadham Green** an estate of large executive homes called Broadham Place has been built on the site of Broadham Mushroom Farm.

Now at the end of the 20C the commercial centre of Oxted has swung from the old High Street to the new Station Roads East and West with modern stores of every kind. But the usual sad process of deterioration in the area left behind has not occurred, because Old Oxted has reinvented itself as a place of specialist businesses and shops against a picturesque background of well-preserved historic buildings and old inns, and it is a living accessory to the commercial centre.

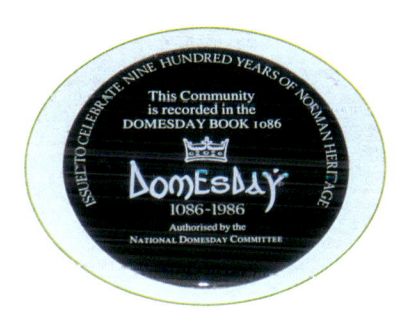

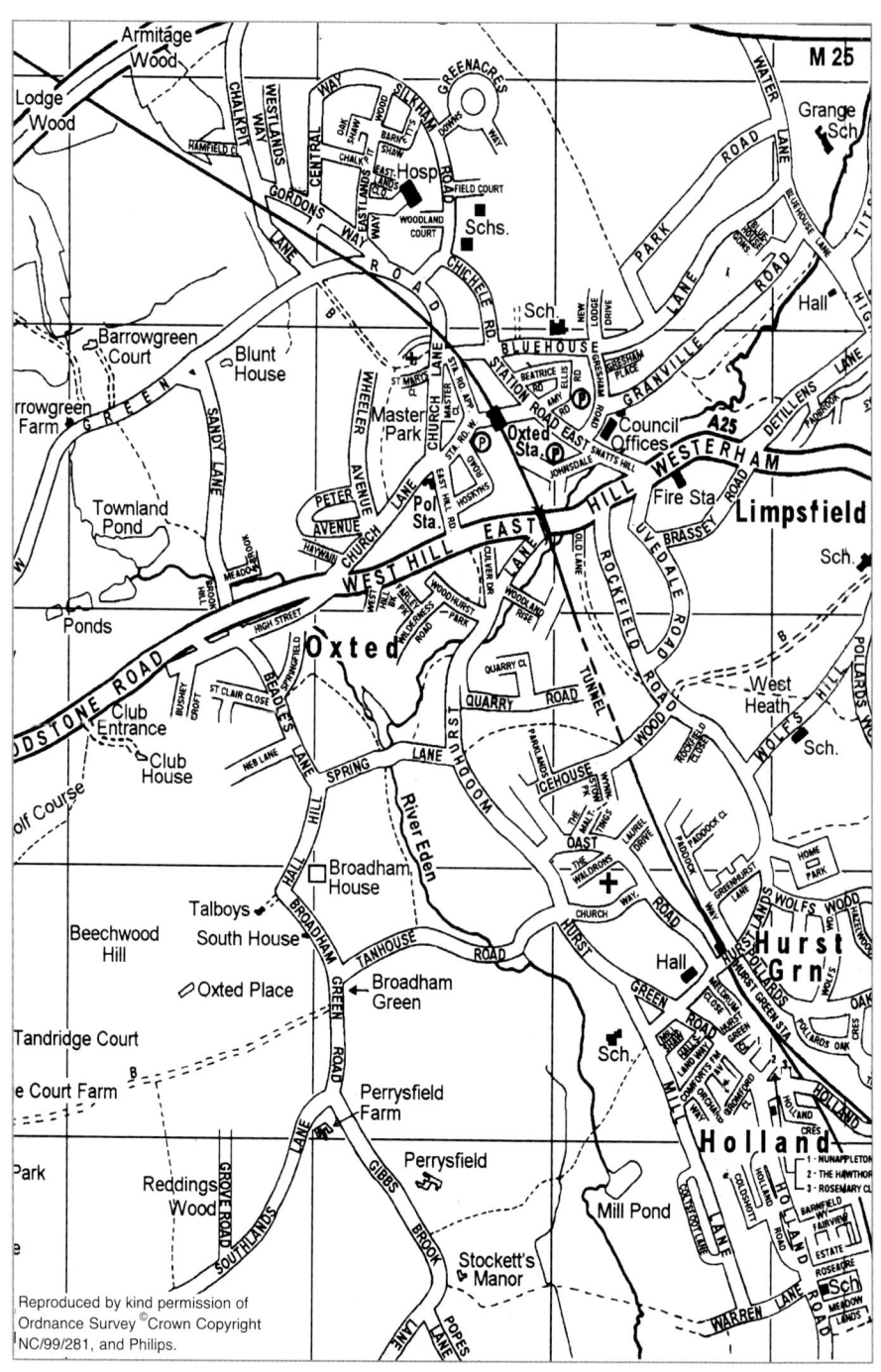

Map of Oxted today

CHAPTER SIX

OXTED TODAY AND INTO THE MILLENNIUM

This chapter describes some of the societies, schools, churches and other institutions and organisations which play a lively role in the life of the town today, though clearly it cannot claim to be exhaustive. Some facilities very much alive and thriving may have been mentioned earlier in the book if the building with which they are associated belongs to architectural history - however modern. Of course, some of these organisations also have a history of their own going back many years which it seems more appropriate to summarise here. These organisations, especially the schools, represent the future, and together with our businesses and shops will carry Oxted forward into the new millennium.

Oxted is now on the Internet, and some foreign visitors have come here attracted by having seen pictures of the town on line. A list of web sites featuring Oxted will be found at the end of the chapter.

Schools

Oxted School was opened in 1929 as Oxted Secondary School, the first mixed grammar school in Surrey, which cost £35,000 to build. In the first term it had 22 pupils, and two years later the numbers had increased to 120. (See also Chapter Five for early memories of the school.) It was designed to grow to 250 pupils, and in the early 30s one writer hoped 'that the full accommodation of 250 will be utilised before long'. In 1932 there was a headmaster and five graduate teachers, with visiting teachers coming in to take classes in Art, Carpentry and Domestic Science. Now in the year 2000 it has over 2000 pupils and 120 staff and is the fourth largest in the country.

In the early hours of 16 August 1998 there was a devastating fire in which 22 classrooms, library, dining-hall and other parts were destroyed, with huge quantities of books and 125 computers. It took 65 firemen four hours to subdue the blaze. With heroic efforts from all concerned, the school reopened in September in temporary classrooms quickly nicknamed The Village. A new building which will be appropriately named the Meridian Building and will contain 24 classrooms, library and dining-room, is scheduled to open on the first day of term in January 2000.

St Mary's School in Silkham Road

St Mary's School was founded in 1872 in Beadles Lane (see Chapter Four), being called Oxtead National Schools and later Beadles Lane County First School. Another part was built in Silkham Road in 1963, and by 1974 the whole school was able to be accommodated at Silkham Road. It now has 360 pupils and maintains close links with St Mary's Church.

Moor House School is a mixed boarding school for children with severe specific speech and language impairment. The original Victorian house (now demolished) with 6.5 acres of land opened in 1947 as a 'school for speech therapy' taking pupils from all over the country, and was probably the first such school in the world. Fees of £5 5s. per week were paid by the local authorities which referred the children to Moor House. The following year there were 38 children, and by 1951 there were 50, for whom the first of many new buildings and extensions had to be constructed. Now there are 87 pupils, aged from seven to 16. The Queen Mother is the patron of the school. The school's fame and reputation has grown over the years and it has international links. It has served as a pioneer in the treatment of speech disorders, and specialists from all over the world have come to study its innovative methods. John Lea, the school's third principal, devised the Colour Pattern Scheme which continues to be widely used to help with the acquisition of grammar skills. Major refurbishments were undertaken in 1999, and there are plans to build a state-of-the-art Sports Hall/Drama Centre at the beginning of the new millennium.

Laverock School was started in 1929, so it has just been celebrating its 70th birthday. It moved to its present site in 1936 where new buildings and up-to-date facilities have been added over the years. It used to be a P.N.E.U. school for both girls and boys - now it takes girls from age 3 to 11.

Downs Way Primary School opened in 1969 with 55 pupils. So in 1999 they celebrated their 30th anniversary, and now they have over 150 children aged from four to seven in six classes. **Limpsfield Grange** was built in 1888. In 1952 it became a school for children with learning difficulties.

Hurst Green County Primary opened in 1960 to cater for the expansion of housing in the area, and opened a nursery in 1993, while further south **Holland Junior School** is a post-war school purpose-built as a Middle School for children from eight to 11, which was opened in 1971. Then in 1993 it became a Junior School for pupils of seven to ten. In 1996 it had a major refit both inside and out.

Churches

Several churches in Oxted work together under the appropriate title 'Churches Together in Oxted and District' and arrange services and other events as joint ventures. *The Oxted Review* is published once a month to give news of churches and general interest articles on the locality.

All Saints Catholic Chutch

The Church of the Peace of God, United Reformed Church

Methodist Church, Hurst Green

The Parish Church, **St Mary's**, has a very long history and this will be found in Chapter Two. Today it is part of a united benefice with St Peter's in Tandridge, in its turn part of the Godstone deanery and under the aegis of the Bishop of Croydon. It is a busy community with a full programme of services and activities, as indeed have all the churches.

All Saints Catholic Church is in Chichele Road, hidden behind the priest's house. The house was bought just before World War I by Father Algernon Lang who was independently wealthy and had been invited by the bishop to establish a parish in Oxted. The first Mass was celebrated in a garden shed on 14 April 1914. The Council did not like Father Lang's idea of building a church beside the house, so he bought the plot behind and the foundation stone was laid the same year. It was finished in 1921 and consecrated in 1927. The only entrance for many years was through the lych-gate behind, which was built in 1927. The church is now a Grade II listed building. A program of expansion is in hand for the millennium when the unusual neo-Gothic rood-screen will be moved from in front of the altar to the rear, thus opening up the interior. The west entrance will be moved back to accommodate more seats, a new porch and sacristy.

St John's, Hurst Green

St Sylvan's Chapel, Staffhurst Wood

First Church of Christ Scientist

The Church of the Peace of God, the United Reformed Church in Bluehouse Lane, was built by the architect Frederic Lawrence in 1935. (The United Reformed Church was formed in 1972 by the union of the Presbyterian Church in England and the Congregational Church in England and Wales.) This replaced the neo-Gothic style Congregational Church built in 1905 which was in Station Road East, approximately where the car showrooms are today. It is hoped that the church can be extended in the near future.

St John's, Hurst Green, was designed by J. Oldrid Scott in neo-Gothic style and opened in 1913. It was enlarged by J. Douglas Matthews in 1962 by one bay, and with a parish room and porch area. It was damaged by fire in 1988, and was restored in 1990, when the opportunity was taken to change the interior, with the altar brought forward and with new chairs. The church hall of St John's is St Agatha's Hall, whose history is related in Chapter Four.

The **Methodist Church**, Hurst Green, is unusual in that it started with a newspaper advertisement in 1958 enquiring whether anyone would be interested in forming a Methodist Society. Hurst Green was chosen as the appropriate venue because of the new housing developments there, and after three years of planning and fund-raising the church was built and opened in 1961. The architect was M.E. Pache and the building firm was R. Durtnell and Sons, a company which has been in the business locally since 1591. In 1998 a vivid new cross-shaped window was installed in the gabled end facing the road.

Other religious communities in the parish include the **Religious Society of Friends** (Quakers), East Hill Road, the **First Church of Christ Scientist**, Church Lane, **St Silvan's**, Staffhurst Wood, the **Evangelical Church**, Hurst Green, **Beadles Lane Chapel** and the **King's Church** which meets in Oxted School.

Organisations

Newcomers to Oxted are provided with *The Link Directory*, listings of services and businesses in the area. The **Link Association** is a charity run by over 200 volunteers, which exists to provide a service for those in need of help, especially with transport and shopping.

Oxted and Limpsfield Hospital was opened in the late 1930s. This was to replace the Oxted and Limpsfield (Memorial) Cottage Hospital built to commemorate local people who served in World War I. The cottage hospital was on the site where Tandridge District Council Offices now are, but eventually it proved inadequate and the present hospital was begun on land donated by the Hoskins Master family. Construction costs came from local fund-raising in which people would buy a brick, or collect a mile of pennies. The hospital provided casualty, out-patient and in-patient care (including a wide range of surgical operations). In 1948 the NHS took it over before the planned maternity unit could be built. Sadly, the hospital could not keep pace with new technology, as funds were directed to Redhill and East Surrey, so that the operating theatre had to be closed.

Now a new hospital is planned with a modern out-patient facility and an adjacent nursing home which will also contain NHS beds. To preserve the link with the memorial nature of the hospital services in Oxted, the old boards of commemoration will be positioned in the new hospital.

Before the Health Centre was built the local GPs held surgeries at their homes and there were two branch surgeries. From the 1970s the Health Centre has provided an integrated service, with more facilities being added all the time, for example, the GPs have been able to take on the running of the state-of-the-art ultrasonic scanner recently given by the League of Friends. The League of Friends provide also a unique service outside the walls of the hospital - this is the only hospital in Surrey where volunteers look after the flowerbeds on the five acres of land.

The Rotary Club of Oxted was founded in 1923 as the 117th club in the country, started by a 'meeting of gentlemen' in the Hoskins Arms Hotel. A collection for charity was made at the weekly lunches - that was in the days when a good lunch cost a Rotarian 2s.6d. (12.5p). Conditions were strict, for irregular attendance at the meetings called down the general wrath of the club, while the poor secretary on at least one occasion was 'severely reprimanded'. But an enormous amount of good work was achieved, orphans were taken on outings, summer camps were offered to city children, with an increase of activity during the war, providing comforts at the searchlight station and supplying canteens. The good work continues today, and has every semblance of continuing into the millennium.

Other organisations serving the community include the **Lions Club**, the **Round Table**, the **Women's Royal Voluntary Service**, the **Royal British Legion**, the **British Red Cross**, the **Citizen's Advice Bureau**, **Age Concern**, **Inner Wheel**, **Rotoract** and many more.

The **Chamber of Commerce**, founded in 1957, represents the businesses of the town. Among many other considerations, they concern themselves with, for example, any planning cases which might have an effect on commercial life. They make sure that shoppers are guided to the stores, and that they are encouraged to choose to come to Oxted by not having to pay for car-parking. The Chamber initiated the idea of hanging flower baskets in Station Road East, and the festive and colourful Christmas lights which for many years have been the responsibility of Mr Terry Tomlinson. At one time streets were closed on a day in December to create a Christmas atmosphere, with Christmas stalls and side shows. Mr Stanley Gibson, chairman of the Chamber for five years, also remembers when the streets were devoted to a summer gala day, with a vintage car parade, Morris dancers and school choirs to entertain the shoppers.

The Limpsfield, Oxted and District Horticultural Society was founded in 1889, so they celebrated their centenary in 1989. The change in the membership of the society over the years reflects the change in the nature of Oxted itself. For example, in the early days many professional gardeners were employed at substantial houses with estates and large gardens, but as Oxted expanded with many more but smaller homes, so the character of the membership changed. The society has managed to keep some old documents which illustrate their history. In 1929 one of their vice-presidents was Sir Ernest Benn of publishing fame, and in that year their autumn show was held in the newly built Barn Theatre, when the highest prize was 10s. In 1937 the subscription was raised from 2s. to 2s.6d. Although the subscription has risen somewhat since then, the society still flourishes.

The Oxted and District History Society was founded in 1960 and now has over 100 members who meet once a fortnight at the Red Cross hall. The subjects of the talks, many illustrated with slides, range from prehistory to modern times and from local history to world developments. Members of the Society have been exceedingly helpful in the preparation of this book.

Holland and District Horticultural Society serves the southern part of the area, while for flower arrangers, the **Oxted and Limpsfield Flower Society** has been going since 1955.

The Women's Institute has several groups in the district and runs a market in the Red Cross hall every Thursday morning.

The **Scouts and Guides** are active too, with groups for Cubs (boys from age 8) Scouts (boys from age 10 $1/2$), and Venture Scouts (boys and girls from 15$1/2$). There is a new experimental section for boys and girls from 14$1/2$. Oxted has one of the oldest Scout groups in the world, since it was founded in 1910, only two years after the formation of the scout movement. There is also the **Hurst Green Scout Group**, and for **Guides** there are two groups in Oxted and two in Hurst Green. **Harry's Youth Centre** in the old Walsted Cottages of 1887 provides facilities and activities for young people.

The **Oxted and Limpsfield Music Society** was formed in 1946. They meet at Hazelwood School four times a year and also in private houses. Famous musicians who have played for them include Moura Lympany, John Lill, Shura Cherkassky, the Amadeus Quartet and Benjamin Britten with Peter Pears. Many other societies cater for varied musical interests, including the **Hurst Green Singers**, the **Oxted and Limpsfield Choral Society**, the **Oxted Orchestral Ensemble** and the **Silver Band** and **Brass Band**.

Other interests are catered for in the **Bridge Clubs**, the **Oxted Art Group** and many others. Courses in **Adult Education** take place in Oxted School and Oxted Library. These are now run by East Surrey College which has taken over from Surrey County Council.

Health and Leisure

Footpaths wind their way over the Downs and beyond. The chalky southern slopes of the North Downs have provided tracks and footways since prehistoric times. The **Pilgrims' Way** has been the romantic name for the ancient track from Winchester to Canterbury and Dover (see Chapter One). However, much of the Way has been obscured in one way or another, has become farmland or private estate, or taken over by busy roads. Thus the idea for the **North Downs Way** arose as part of a grander network in the minds of planners since 1947. It took another 30 years to achieve and the North Downs Way was officially opened in 1978. North of Oxted the Pilgrims' Way and the North Downs Way run quite closely together. From the A22 eastwards they coincide for a while until they are nearly at the railway tunnel where the North Downs Way goes to the north of the Pilgrims' Way. Then they come together for a short distance until the Pilgrims' Way goes through Titsey Park so the North Downs Way again swings to the north and stays there for many miles. The Pilgrims' Way takes to a surfaced road - Pilgrims' Lane - at Titsey Church and passes a farm called Pilgrims' Farm.

The **Greensand Way** is an unofficial footpath across Surrey, opened in 1982, and marked on some maps. It runs to the south of the A25 and passes between Oxted and Hurst Green. A spur through Oxted links it to the North

Downs Way. You will also see **Vanguard Way** on maps, crossing near Oxted. It links Croydon and the coast.

Tandridge Leisure Pool, mentioned in the last chapter, has a swimming pool and adjoining 'lagoon' with waves, jacuzzi, sauna, gym, crèche, children's activities, exercise classes and a coffee bar. There are about 40 **Sports Clubs** operating in the district, catering for over 20 different types of sport, from Angling down through the alphabet to Walking.

Entertainment

The Mock Tudor **Plaza Cinema** described in the last chapter still shows the latest most popular films.

The **Barn Theatre** plans radical improvements, the first phase will be the new car-park. Then, on the east side the theatre will be extended to provide a large new green room, new bar and an internal stair to the gallery at present accessed from outside. Toilet facilities for the disabled will be backstage and near the foyer, and wheelchair access to the stage will be possible from the dressing-rooms. There will be full height wing space with external loading,

Oxted Inn and Station

another dressing-room and scenery paint shop. Patrons of the new plan are Ronnie Corbett, Richard Stilgoe, Judi Dench and her husband Michael Williams, and Peter Ainsworth MP.

We have now followed the history of Oxted from its hazy beginnings in Saxon times to its mention in the historic Domesday Book, and from a medieval village of stately hall houses to a thriving 19C town. We have charted the upheaval brought by the railway and the establishment of New Oxted. Through a thousand years, Oxted has shown the two essential traits of adaptability and resilience, and come to its own individual twentieth-century identity by means of a unique partnership - an attractive commercial centre linked to a medieval street. Here new specialist businesses have been established, and the old inns still provide good fare and a convivial atmosphere. In this last chapter we have presented the ways in which the people of this community interact to provide a lively social and commercial scene, with opportunities for everyone to fulfil his or her physical, cultural and spiritual needs. Now at the end of 1999 Oxted is ready to enter the new millennium, to grasp new opportunities and at the same time to continue to serve its people well.

Internet sites

Oxted general: http://www.knowhere.co.uk/479.html

Oxted School: http://schoolsite.edex.net.uk/288/frames.htm

Oxted Pubs:
http://www.camrabranches.org.uk/surrey/pubguide/oxted/pubentry.htm

There are several other special interest and commercial sites to be found as well.

FURTHER READING

Antiquities and Conservation Areas of Surrey published by Surrey County Council. 1976

Continuing History of the Barn Theatre by Stanley Brown.

Churches of Surrey by Mervyn Blatch. 1997

Early Medieval Surrey by John Blair. 1991

History and Antiquities of the County of Surrey by Manning and Bray. 1809

Inventory of Buildings of Historic Interest in Oxted by Peter Gray (forthcoming)

List of Monumental Brasses in Surrey by Mills Stephenson. 1970

'Literary' Oxted and Limpsfield by Robin Peel. 1984

Manor of Oxted by W.F. Mumford. Vol. 63, Surrey Archaeological Collections. 1966

Natural History and Antiquities of Surrey by John Aubrey. 1719

Oxted Explored by Annette Wells and Kay Percy. 1975

Oxted, Limpsfield and Neighbourhood ed. by Lewis G. Fry. 1932

Oxted Line by R.W. Kidner. 1981

Oxted in Old Picture Postcards Vol 1 & 2 by Roger Packham. 1987 and 1990

Pages from the Past in Oxted, Limpsfield and Tandridge by W.F. Mumford. 1949

Surrey (Buildings of England Series) by Ian Nairn and Nikolaus Pevsner. 1971

Topographical History of the County of Surrey by Edward Brayley. 2nd ed. 1878

Victoria County History: Surrey. 1912

Watermills of Surrey by Derek Stiddler. 1990